Father Boero

The Jesuit Martyre of Japan

A History of the Lives and Martyrdom of Paul Michi

Father Boero

The Jesuit Martyre of Japan
A History of the Lives and Martyrdom of Paul Michi

ISBN/EAN: 9783337183714

Printed in Europe, USA, Canada, Australia, Japan

Cover: Foto ©Lupo / pixelio.de

More available books at **www.hansebooks.com**

THE JESUIT MARTYRS OF JAPAN.

A HISTORY

OF

THE LIVES AND MARTYRDOM

OF

PAUL MICHI,
JAMES CHISAI, AND JOHN SOAN DE GOTO,
OF THE SOCIETY OF JESUS:

BY FATHER BOERO,
OF THE SAME SOCIETY.

TRANSLATED FROM THE ITALIAN
BY A CATHOLIC PRIEST.

DUBLIN:
JAMES DUFFY, 7, WELLINGTON-QUAY,
AND 22, PATERNOSTER-ROW, LONDON.
1862.

CONTENTS.

PREFACE, ... vii

FIRST PART.

                                                                          PAGE

I. Life of the Holy Martyr, Paul Michi, his country, birth, and childhood, . . 1

II. His education in the seminary of the nobles in Anzuciama, ... 5

III. Paul runs great risk of his life during the sack of Anzuciama—He pursues his studies, ... 9

IV. He enters the Society of Jesus, and applies himself to the acquirement of human and divine knowledge, ... 14

V. His missionary labours and apostolic preaching, ... 18

VI. His writings and publications in defence of the faith, ... 23

VII. A short account of his religious virtues, . 25

VIII. Life of the holy Martyr John Soan or de Goto—His country and birth—Goes into voluntary exile for the faith, . . . 29

IX. Asks to be received into the Society—Is made Catechist—System of selecting them—His labours with Father Peter de Morecon, ... 32

X. The life of the holy Martyr James Chisai—Born and reared a heathen, he is converted to the faith of Jesus Christ—He marries and repudiates his wife on account of her apostacy from the faith, . . 37

XI. He renounces the world, and goes to live with the Fathers of the Society as Catechist—His tender devotion to the Passion of Jesus Christ, ... 39

SECOND PART.

Passion and Death of the Three Holy Martyrs.

I. Foundation of Christianity in Japan—Character of the Emperor Taicosama, . . 43

II. Taicosama's first persecution of the Christians—Origin of another and more terrible persecution—He sentences all the ministers and followers of the Gospel to death, 47

III. Zeal of the Christians in presenting themselves for martyrdom—Taicosama mitigates his sentence against the Fathers and the faithful, ... 54

IV. Taicosama sentences the religious to death—A curious incident of one man substituting himself for another of the same name in order to win the palm of martyrdom, ... 67

V. How our three, Paul Michi, John de Goto, and James Chisai, were comprised in the sentence of death—the wonderful delight with which they accept martyrdom, . 73

CONTENTS.

PAGE

VI. The Japanese executioner cuts off an ear of each of the twenty-four martyrs—They are exposed to public derision in the streets of Miako—Affecting incident of an old man recently converted to the faith, ... 79

VII. Father Organtino's sentiments on receiving the ears of our three brothers—How the Martyrs comported themselves in the streets of Miako, ... 88

VIII. The Martyrs are conveyed from Miako to Nangasasky—Incidents on the way, . 96

IX. They are joined by new companions on the way—The Martyrs arrive at Facata—Letters from the Commissary, Peter Baptist and Paul Michi, addressed to the Rector of Nangasasky and the Viceprovincial, ... 104

X. Discovery of miraculous crucifixes presaging martyrdom on the cross, . . . 112

XI. Various incidents connected with the Martyrs in the vicinity of Nangasasky—Fazamburo's affection for Paul Michi—Paul's joy and fervor—John Soan and James Chisai make their religious vows—Respect shown to the Martyrs by the Christians—John's interview with his father, ... 120

XII. Japanese crosses.—How the Japanese crucify their criminals—Interesting incidents relating to the twenty-six crucified Martyrs—Paul Michi addresses the spectators from his cross, ... 143

	PAGE
XIII. Concourse and devotion of the Christians to the Martyrs—They are visited and venerated by the Bishop of Japan, the King of Arima, and the Prince of Omura,	158
XIV. Wonderful signs in confirmation of their martyrdom; and, above all, how their blood became the seed of vast numbers of Christians,	165
XV. Translation of the Martyrs' relics to Manilla and Macao—Acts of their canonization,	169
XVI. Catalogue of the religious of the Society put to death for the faith in Japan—Brief notice of the Bishops who governed that Church,	172
Decree of the Sacred Congregation of Rites for the canonization of the twenty-six Martyrs,	183
Decree of the Holiness of our Lord Pius IX., sanctioning the canonization of the three Martyrs of the Society of Jesus,	ib.

PREFACE.

For sake of greater clearness, I divide this brief history into two parts. In the first I will give the life of the three holy Martyrs, taking it from authentic and trustworthy memoirs, and also from the more elaborate writings of Nierembergh, Alegambe, the Bollandists, and other authors. In the second part I will narrate the causes which originated the persecution; and under the same head I will recount distinctly the Acts of the Martyrs, in the very words of that most exquisite and elegant narrative which has been handed down to us by Father Daniel Bartoli, in his *History of Japan.*

It is, therefore, not without good reason that I have called this book not a history written by myself, but a *compilation*, with a view that everything that is good or valuable in it may be reflected back on the unparalleled genius and most elegant style of Bartoli. I will say nothing of the veracity or fidelity of his narrative; for he has drawn all the particulars from the sacred and civil informations, which were authentically deposed, concerning this memorable fact, by order of the Sacred Congregation of Rites, and the Royal Court of Spain, as also from letters and original reports which were despatched by ocular witnesses from Japan to Rome, all of which we still preserve.

May the Lord deign to regard with merciful eyes that abandoned nation, and cause the blood of its thousands of martyrs to fructify speedily! Martyrs indeed they were, who, in the midst of the most atrocious torments and afflictions, generously defended the faith of Jesus Christ, carried thither by the Apostle of the East, Saint Francis Xavier—nay, cultivated and disseminated it throughout the whole empire, till at last it was entirely uprooted and destroyed by the fury of persecutions.

THE LIVES

OF THE

HOLY MARTYRS OF JAPAN.

LIFE OF THE HOLY MARTYR, PAUL MICHI—HIS COUNTRY, BIRTH, AND CHILDHOOD.

JAPAN, an empire in the most eastern part of Asia, consists of a group of islands situated at short distances from one another, and was discovered by the Portuguese in 1542. These islands communicate with each other by means of inlets from the sea; the principal being eight in number, and three of these, Niphon, Xicoco, and Ximo, the largest, occupy an area considerably greater than that of all Italy. The principal island, which the natives call Niphon, the Chinese Ippon, and we Japan, gives its name to the whole of that Archipelago. Japan was anciently governed by an emperor, called the Dairi, or Ecclesiastical Sovereign; but when the governors of the provinces rebelled against his authority, they divided the empire into sixty-six, or, as others say, sixty-eight petty principalities, till at last, some time before the year 1571, Nobunanga, prince of a minor province named Voari, by force of arms made himself monarch of thirty-five kingdoms; and Fasciba, his successor, consolidated all Japan under one monarchy, which has continued down to our times.

It was in this kingdom that our holy martyr, Paul Michi, was born, in the year 1564. Documents forwarded to Rome by the Jesuit Provincial of Japan, fully satisfy us that he saw the light in Giamascir, a district bordering on the grand Miako, then the metropolis, or chief seat of the government of the entire kingdom. His father was Michi Fandoidono, a man of most noble descent, famed for his martial career, and for a long time before greatly esteemed by the emperor Nobunanga, in whose court he resided. His mother, who in baptism was called Mary, was also of noble blood, for it is an inflexible law of the Japanese that their nobility shall never intermarry with persons of inferior social position. It was in all probability in the court of Miako that they became acquainted with the Jesuits, and it was there also, in the year 1568, that they both embraced the Christian faith, which they unswervingly professed to the end of their lives. In that same year they also consecrated their child to God—he being then five years old—giving him at the regenerating fountain the name of Paul. Thus did grace take up its abode in that innocent soul, even in his tenderest years, and thus did it watch over the days of his childhood, a period of life exposed to many dangers in those regions where idolatry was so universal, every vice so contagious, and most of all, that of lasciviousness. The special providence of Heaven, and the tender solicitude of his pious parents caused the little Paul to increase in years and in the holy fear of God; for, even at that early period of his life, he was singularly remarkable for the fervour of his devotion, gravity, and modesty of demeanour, amiability of manners, submission, and obedience.

At length his parents finding that they could not devote sufficient time to the instruction of their child—the mother being constantly occupied with household affairs, and the father almost always in the camp or in the court—made up their minds to confide his education in piety and learning to Father Organtino Soldi, who was then in Miako, and who may be justly styled the father of Christianity in that distant region; for he was, indeed, a man of most holy life and glowing zeal, of whom his native city, Brescia, has reason to be proud, but more so still the Society of Jesus, that was his parent, and sent him to Japan, where he was employed thirty-six years in the constant labours of the apostolic ministry. This holy man willingly undertook to educate Paul, then a youth in his eleventh year, and kept him for some time under his immediate care, till at length he found opportunity of placing him, with other boys of noble birth, in a seminary or boarding house, which he had founded and opened, and which worked admirably for the diffusion of the faith.

II.

HIS EDUCATION IN THE SEMINARY OF THE NOBLES IN ANZUCIAMA.

THE emperor Nobunanga, to immortalise his name, had erected from the foundations a new city and fortress in Anzuciama, a most delightful region, situated on the frontier of the kingdom of Voari, and within about fourteen leagues of Miako. The Christians of that city justly thought, that it would be an inestimable advantage to the faith, if the Fathers of the Society would be allowed to open a church and residence in that new seat of royalty, where the princes and chiefs of more than thirty districts, subjects to Nobunanga, were in the habit of meeting and residing the greater part of the year. Conscious of the great good that would result from such a state of things, they, therefore, begged Father Organtino to present a memorial to the emperor (who, for some time back, had shown himself rather well affected to the Christian law), embodying their wishes for leave to erect a church and dwelling-house. The good father had an audience of Nobunanga, and got from that monarch far more than what he asked—a large subsidy in money and a site for the sacred edifice, which the emperor directed to be built opposite to his own palace. This concession obtained, Father Organtino immediately took asunder a large wooden house that he had raised at Miako, and with the assistance of the Christians—multitudes of whom willingly gave their services—he transported it to Anzuciama, and with it twenty-five noble youths, among them Paul Michi, whom he had already selected for his seminary. These were soon joined by others—many of them of royal blood—who, being provided with experienced masters and teachers, commenced to study the Latin and Japanese languages, devoting themselves at the same time to serving in the church, and to other works of singular piety and devotion. In fact, such was the reputation of these holy youths, that they attracted many of the principal men of the country to visit them frequently, nay, and to hold conferences with the Fathers concerning God and their souls. Whenever the seminarists went out two by two into the streets, the people crowded after them admiring them, and thanking heaven for the sight of such modesty and decorum; so much so, that Nobunanga himself—forgetful, as it were, of the more than human pride in which he was habitually wrapped—often visited the seminary, accompanied by a small retinue, and, with condescension never shown even to the most exalted of his courtiers, conversed with the pupils, who welcomed him with an exhibition of their advancement in various branches of knowledge, and the harmonious sounds of foreign instruments, on which they had been taught to perform.

Owing to such favourable auspices all these youths, but two particularly, were enabled to render great services towards propagating the faith, and these were Jerom, son of the prince of Fungo, nephew of the holy king Francis of Bungo, and our Paul Michi. Jerom had been selected to go to Rome in the quality of chief ambassador to tender obedience to the Holy See, but as the ships were on the point of sailing before he could possibly reach the port of Nangasasky, Ito Mantio, his cousin, was substituted in his stead. The latter subsequently adopted the military profession, and distinguished himself highly by his valorous exploits; but far more glorious is his name in the church of Japan for his most exemplary Christian life, and the invincible fidelity with which he clung to the faith to the latest moment of his life. Paul, who was of gentler nature, showed a decided vocation for the ecclesiastical state, and was constantly intent on acquiring knowledge and piety, in order that he might be enabled to devote himself entirely to God and the salvation of souls. In course of time his holy aspirations were realised; and here let us remark, that if the noble college of Anzuciama, during its short-lived existence, had produced only these two zealous champions of the faith, it would deserve to be regarded as having eminent claims on the gratitude of the Japanese Church.

III.

PAUL RUNS GREAT RISKS OF HIS LIFE DURING THE SACK OF ANZUCIAMA—HE PURSUES HIS STUDIES.

PAUL had not been two years in Anzuciama when an occurrence took place which changed the whole state of civil affairs, and was near involving him, his companions, and the Jesuit Fathers in most imminent peril of their lives.

Let us narrate the facts. Acheci, prince of a small territory, having, through motives of ambition, rebelled against Nobunanga, entered Miako with the flower of his army on the night of the 20th of June, 1582, and suddenly surrounding Nobunanga's palace, proceeded with a band of conspirators to assassinate the emperor. The latter, however, having sometime before been wounded, fled to hide himself in a secret chamber where, in order to escape the ignominy of falling into the hands of his enemies after death, he set fire to the palace, then inflicted a mortal wound on his abdomen, and died of self-murder. After taking Miako, the rebels marched on Anzuciama, which they had hardly reached when the garrison surrendered to them on conditions and the citizens at discretion. It may be imagined how desperate was the condition of our religious at that period, when the soldiery were scouring the streets killing all who came in their way, and the fire which broke out in various quarters was destroying the ill-fated city. Abandoning the Residence, Father Organtino took our Paul and the other students along with him to the shore of the lake that spread out before the palace, and with great difficulty succeeded in hiring a boat. This, however, was only exchanging one danger for another; for, as they had entrusted themselves to an idolatrous robber, who was owner of the boat, and who rowed them to Vachimoscima, a little island ten miles up the lake, the perfidious villain, regardless of his word, there robbed them of everything they had, and was preparing to carry them off to another uninhabited island, doubtless, with the intention of murdering them all. But God's special providence watched over those twenty-eight souls; for, a Christian nobleman, as it were inspired by heaven, hastened in an armed vessel to their rescue, and taking them out of the robber's hands brought them to Sacomote, where, through a merciful dispensation, they got a written protection from one of Acheci's sons, and a page who acted as guide till they arrived, after many hair-breadth escapes, safely in Miako.

During all these bitter trials nothing could be more admirable than the tranquillity and collectedness of Paul, who, instead of seeking a sure asylum under his parents' roof, as he might have done, preferred rather, for the love of Christ, to share the fortunes of the Fathers, among whom it was his dearest wish to be enrolled. He remained but a short time in Miako; for, about twelve days after Nobunanga's death, the traitor Acheci was routed and slain by Guisto Ucondono, prince of Tacatzuchi, and a most zealous Christian, who caused the seminary to be removed to his country. Paul, therefore, proceeded thither to resume his studies. His chiefest and most delightful pursuit was to indoctrinate himself profoundly in the mysteries of the faith, and familiarize himself with everything that concerned the apostolic ministry. Such, also, was the grand object of the Fathers in training the youths committed to their care—in other words, to make them catechists, clerics, lay brothers, and priests, who, in course of time, would be able to diffuse the faith, and confute the errors of the idolatrous sectaries. The master who had charge of these youths was one of our Japanese lay brothers, named Vincent, a most profound reasoner, who, by dint of long study, had so completely mastered the secret theology of the Bonzes, or idalatrous priests, that many of the most learned of the latter and their pupils came from far off regions and their most renowned schools, to confer with him. Many of them returned to their respective countries Christians, and from slaves of error and superstition became teachers of the faith. It is easy to imagine how great was the progress which Paul made under such a system of training; and, indeed, his after-life proved that he became one of the most powerful orators and able apologists that the Jesuits had in Japan. During his sojourn in Tacatzuchi, and afterwards in Arima—whither, on account of more recent revolutions, the

Fathers were obliged to remove the seminary—he would accompany the priests on their missions, catechizing the neophytes, engaging the Bonzes in controversy, and occasionally, as we find it recorded, reciting his sermons in the church with a graceful eloquence, that might not have been expected from one so young.

IV.

HE ENTERS THE SOCIETY OF JESUS, AND APPLIES HIMSELF TO THE ACQUIREMENT OF HUMAN AND DIVINE KNOWLEDGE.

A soul so well inclined, was not destined for worldly pursuits; and Paul's dearest ambition was to be received into our Society, from whose Superiors he begged this boon with never-ceasing importunity. They, however, had to act with great caution, nor could they be induced to receive the Japanese into the Order till they had been well tested and trained under their own eyes in the duties of catechists. Paul's case, however, was one of peculiar character; for, he had been baptized in childhood, educated in our seminaries, reared by our missionaries, and then the death of his father, Fandoidono, who fell gloriously in this year (1586) fighting under the banner of Francis, king of Bungo, against Satzuma (an idolator); determined the Fathers to comply with his pious request. He was, therefore, received into the Society, and in the August of the same year (1586), he was sent to our novitiate of All Saints, near Nangasasky, having then attained his twenty-second year.

Henceforth, his grand aim was to strengthen himself with these solid virtues which he would be called upon to exercise at every moment of his life, amid the labors and trials of that most arduous mission. And, indeed, he found occasion to bring them into action in less than eleven months' time, when Cambacudono, who usurped the empire after Nobunanga's demise, infuriated by a malignant Bonze, all of a sudden became an implacable enemy to the Christians, whom he had hitherto regarded with favor, and issued a proclamation commanding all the ministers of the Gospel to quit his territories. At that period the Jesuits were the only missionaries in Japan, and numbered about one hundred and twenty, besides a great multitude of catechists whom they had in training. Father Gaspar Coeglio, then Viceprovincial, seeing things come to this pass, immediately consulted the Christian kings and princes; and, acting on the advice of the most experienced of them, resolved — in order that the barbarous Cambacudono might not become more exasperated—to make a display of submission, and accordingly lost no time in assembling a crowd of the converts at the harbour of Firando, as though they were ready to embark. His object, however, was to disperse them hither and thither in various places, dressed in the ordinary Japanese costume, that they might thus circumspectly keep the faith alive in those one hundred and fifty thousand Christians, whom we had then in the country, and for whose weal he prescribed salutary regulations. They did as he advised them, betaking themselves to this and that quarter, as circumstances suggested, and our Paul with his brother novices, sought refuge in Arie, a small territory some distance from Arima.

At the close of the two years' noviciate, in the August of 1588, having consecrated himself to God by the three vows of poverty, chastity, and obedience, he was sent to the island of Amacusa, where, under the protection of John, prince of that region, we had then a flourishing university for our young students. Here he revised the entire course through which he had gone in the seminaries, and, as Heaven had blessed him with wonderful intellectual powers, he applied himself to the study of philosophy and theology, speculative, moral, and controversial. Nor should we omit mentioning that he devoted a considerable amount of time and unwearied diligence to perusing the superstitious works of the numerous sects with which Japan swarms; his grand object being to condense their errors and contradictions, and to write treatises which would expose the one and confute the other, and supply him with arguments whenever he might have to dispute with the idolators and Bonzes.

V.

HIS MISSIONARY LABOURS AND APOSTOLIC PREACHING.

HAVING completed his course of studies, and armed himself at all points with virtue and learning, Paul at length set out to commence the work on which he had set his heart, namely, to gain souls to Christ. He was thoroughly master of the Japanese language, not only of the vulgar vernacular, but also of the learned idiom in which the upper classes converse; and so profound was his knowledge of it that he made himself master of all its peculiarities, elegancies and pronunciation—things which foreigners find it almost impossible to acquire, even after many years of unwearied and incessant study. He was also blessed with a gift of natural eloquence and grace of diction peculiarly his own, which, deriving additional power from his piety and angelic modesty, charmed, convinced, and softened the hearts of all those who conversed with him. His first essay was in the capacity of catechist, when our Fathers appointed him to instruct the neophytes in the mysteries of the faith, till he was gradually promoted to the office of preacher. The earliest field of his labors was Scimo, that is, the territory and islands situated in the south, and principally the kingdom of Arima, and the principality of Omura, where there was a vast congregation of Christians Proceeding thence northwards, he visited many regions before he arrived at Miako, whence he journeyed fully two hundred miles to the remotest confines of Japan.

He was always accompanied by one or more of our priests. His duty was to preach, instruct, dispute, and prepare the converts for baptism, and that of the priests to administer the sacrament of penance, celebrate the holy sacrifice, solemnize marriages, and comfort the dying." It would be impossible to describe all he had to endure in these long journeys, or to recount the ever-recurring dangers which beset him. All, however, were as nothing in his eyes compared to the rich and abundant harvest which lay before him. It is well known that he was greatly esteemed and loved by the idolatrous princes and chieftains, and that he converted very many of them to the faith of Jesus Christ, particularly in the kingdoms of the Mori. Letters written from that quarter state that our holy faith, during the course of the forty-five years since its first introduction into Japan by St. Francis Xavier, had never made such progress as that which was witnessed in 1593, and the two following years, whether we regard the numbers of the converts, their exalted social position, or the many kingdoms to which their respective potentates invited our missionaries. That the labours of our holy martyr, Paul, contributed largely to bring about such numerous and important conversions, appears not only from the testimony of the Jesuit writers, but also from the statement of Father Marcellus Ribadeneira, of the order of St. Francis, who visited Japan, was personally acquainted with Paul Michi, and has left on record that his energetic exertions produced more abundant fruit than fell to the share of any other.

As an evidence of the power and efficacy of his *preaching*, we will here mention a single fact which has been well authenticated. In the city of Ozaca an unfortunate criminal—an idolator—was sentenced to death, and as he was on the way to the place of execution, it so happened that our saint made his appearance. Inflamed with desire to impart eternal life to the individual who was about to lose the temporal, he forced his way through the crowd and soldiery, and going up the condemned, commenced discoursing with him energetically of the never-ending pains which await those who do not adore the true God of the Christians, and then of the necessity of believing in Jesus Christ and being baptized, in order to obtain everlasting salvation of the soul. This forcible appeal, so generous and so holy, with the aid of divine grace, made due impression on the heart of the unhappy culprit who, on the instant, acknowledged that truth had triumphed over him. Paul instructed him as well as he could on the way to the place of execution, and no sooner had the convert been baptised, than he submitted willingly to his fate; and thus, as we have reason to believe, secured the salvation of his regenerated soul.

VI.

HIS WRITINGS AND PUBLICATIONS IN DEFENCE OF THE FAITH.

Nor was it only with word of mouth that Paul contributed to the propagation of the faith. Quite the contrary, indeed; for, his pen was employed for the same grand object. Thoroughly conversant as he was with the language and peculiar style of writing in use among the Japanese, and equally well skilled in the theological system of the Bonzes, he composed a book that, in elegant diction, exposed the vanity of idols and the errors of the Japanese sects—which, contrasted with the holy and true law of Christ, are nothing more than a jumble of fables, errors, contradictions, principles, and maxims, repugnant to right reason and natural decency. At that period the principal sects which sowed the tares of vice and error among the Japanese were twelve in number, each of them having schools, temples, priests, and preachers. Paul confuted them all one after the other, proving to them, at the same time, the monstrous absurdities of the *Canonical Book* of Japan, which they attribute to Sciaca, an idol held in greatest veneration by the mass of the people. These works were first circulated in manuscript; but as soon as Father Alexander Valegnani, Visitator of the East, introduced the printing press, they were published for general circulation. Thus was our Paul the first of the Japanese, who wrote and published works in defence of Christianity, and hence it is that he is mentioned in the catalogue of our writers as an author of polemic theology. The acts of canonization declare, that by this means he gained innumerable souls to the faith; for he thus extended his zeal to places where he could not be bodily present, nay, and to future times long after his glorious death.

VII.

A SHORT ACCOUNT OF HIS RELIGIOUS VIRTUES.

The zeal with which Paul labored by voice and pen to propagate the Christian religion among his Japanese compatriots, was further enhanced by the efficacy and example of his religious virtues. I will not say much on this head, in order to avoid prolixity. Notwithstanding the distractions attendant on his mission, he was always in close communion with God; and of this intimacy he was wont to speak with tenderness truly affecting, and, indeed, with fervor of spirit. After his long and wearisome missionary journeys, he was in the habit of resting himself (according to the rule prescribed by Father Valegnani, visitator of the East) in some one of our residences; and here for many days his devout soul was still more intensely inflamed by protracted meditations and austere penances. Grave and modest in his deportment, he was amiable and affable in his intercourse with all who approached him. So much so, indeed (as ocular witnesses have testified), that he succeeded in overcoming the prejudices and winning the affections of the idolatrous Bonzes; nay, and even of those who were most opposed to the law of Christ. The Japanese are notorious for two vices—inveterate in their nature—craft, and dissimulation; so much so, that Father Valegnani, in one of his letters to our General, speaks of that benighted people thus:—" Two things I find most intolerable in Japan; one is to have to do with people who never have on their lips what they have in their heart; and all of them are brought up from childhood in that system, and none more so than the upper classes, who deem lying a virtue, and glory in being able to deceive, in order that no one may discover what they intend or wish." How different was Paul! That candor that was in his heart was always on his lips; for, indeed, he was at all times and in all circumstances, honest and guileless. He was indifferent about his life, always provided that it might be the means of gaining a soul to Christ; and what is more, nothing could excel his patience in the midst of sufferings and trials, inseparable from the apostolic ministry; but never so much so as in the time of persecution. "Praise to God," writes one who lived at that period and in that land, "our life is like that which the Apostle describes; for, we go about clothed in skins, afflicted, persecuted, wandering through forests and valleys, and seeking refuge in the caverns of the earth. No rest by night, for it is spent in visiting our converts, preaching to them, and administering the Sacraments. When day comes, we hide ourselves as well as we can, or, at all events, keep away from the inhabited regions." And this, indeed, is but a faint picture of the life which our Paul had to lead for many a year during the first persecution inflicted on the Christians by king Taicosama. But to be short, I will now confine myself to laying before the reader the elegant eulogium which Father Marcellus Ribadeneira, already mentioned, has pronounced on our Paul, in his history of the Archipelago:—" I have known him," says that writer, "to be a man most observant of silence and modesty. His every act clearly proved how admirably he realised in practice all that religious perfection he imbibed during the eleven years he lived in the Society. The Christians regarded this holy martyr as a most efficient preacher; and it was almost proverbial among them that he did more for the faith than any of his colleagues; for, his zeal did not show itself so much in words as in results. The Fathers of the Society always spoke of him as a good and humble labourer in the missionary field; one, in a word, who sought nothing but the salvation of his neighbours' souls and his own advancement in virtue." As Paul had now entered on his thirty-third year, the time arrived when he was to be ordained priest by the bishop of Japan, Peter Martinez (of the Society of Jesus), who landed in that country in the year 1596; but before our martyr's aspirations could be gratified,

God decreed that instead of a priest he should become a victim, offered to Christ on the altar of the cross, and venerated as a martyr by the same bishop in the city of Nangasasky, as we will relate after having said something of the lives of the two other saints.

VII.

LIFE OF THE HOLY MARTYR JOHN SOAN, OR DE GOTÒ—HIS COUNTRY AND BIRTH—GOES INTO VOLUNTARY EXILE FOR THE FAITH.

Gotò is a group of islands which, in their entirety constitute a kingdom. They may be said to almost join each other, as there is but a mile and a-half of an inlet from the sea flowing between each of them. These islands are situated some fifty leagues from Firando. The whole of that region is sterile and bare, although it abounds in living springs and a good tract of it is covered with dense forests. Withal, as the Japenese can subsist on little, it has its towns on the level lands and in the mountain ranges there is a numerous population. Ozaca the royal residence, is situated on the sea side, in a very delightful spot; and the city itself, after the fashion of that country, may be said to be magnificent. The faith was introduced into that region by two of our catechists, Louis Almeida, a Portuguese, and one Laurence, a Japanese, who were succeeded by Fathers Monti, of Ferrara, Alexander Valla, of Lombardy, and Joseph Fornaletti, a Venetian, who was put to death (in odium of the faith) by poison. On the conversion, however, of prince Louis, lord of that region, all its inhabitants received baptism.

It was in one of these islands that our holy young martyr, John, was born, in 1578, of parents who had been converted to the faith, and who, as I think, were amongst the first to embrace it. Soan was his paternal cognomen; but as there were, probably, other catechists of the same name, I find him always called DE GOTÒ, from the kingdom of which he was a native. Educated in the Christian religion by his parents, and instructed in the mysteries of the faith by the Fathers of the Society, who were preaching in these islands, he grew up in the holy fear of God, and in the exercise of all virtues. On the death, however, of Prince Louis, one of his brothers, a most fanatical idolator, deeming it a favorable opportunity, collected a force, and wrested the kingdom from the legitimate successor, a mere child, and who was also called Louis. Far from being satisfied with usurpation, this unbeliever, instigated by the Bonzes, raged fearfully against the Christians, many of whom, the most distinguished and wealthy, not being any longer allowed to practise their religion in their own country, went into voluntary exile, and among them the family of Soan. John, therefore, accompanied his parents to Nangasasky, a city then almost entirely Christian, situated on the sea shore, and within the states of Omura. Here the Society had a residence and a church, and the Christians were permitted to exercise their religion openly by a new concession from Taicosama, who did not deem it politic to disgust the Portuguese, who made the place an entreport for their traffic with India and China. The child being thus provided with greater aids for his soul's advancement, made wonderful progress in virtue, and gave an unmistakable proof of proficiency by withdrawing altogether from the world, in order that he might consecrate himself to God.

VIII.

ASKS TO BE RECEIVED INTO THE SOCIETY.—IS MADE CATECHIST.—SYSTEM OF SELECTING THEM. HIS LABOURS WITH FATHER PETER DE MORECON.

CONSTANT intercourse with the Fathers stimulated him to imitate their lives; so much so, indeed, that, when little more than fifteen years of age, he besought the Viceprovincial to receive him into the order. His request was, in some measure, granted, for he was enrolled among the catechists, which was the first step, and the first probation, in order to be received as a religious. To the end that we may appreciate the dignity and status of the catechists, it is necessary to observe that, with a view to render that office more desirable, and those who exercise it more venerable, as a class engaged in a holy work, the Fathers had instituted, if I may so express myself, a solemn form of ordaining them, with a ceremony like that used when giving the habit to religious. The selected persons, therefore, or accepted, were either boys not under ten years of age, or youths more advanced, not excluding men of riper years, who were single. The qualifications required were holiness of life, fervent zeal, intellectual ability, and good reasoning capabilities; while, at the same time, the Fathers set great value on those who abandoned their homes and parents, in order to consecrate themselves to God. Indeed, many of those whose fathers and mothers were living were presented by the latter to the service of the Church on some festival day. When the congregation had assembled, the superior sang Mass, the Portuguese and seminarists (whenever they could be had) performing the sacred music; and after the Gospel one of the Fathers ascended the pulpit, and discoursed on the holy ministry of instructing heathens in the faith, or on some similar subject, and the virtues that should distinguish those who were anxious to exercise it worthily. The sermon concluded, the music was resumed, and the new catechist, kneeling at the foot of the altar, cut off, with his own hand, that tuft of hair which the Japanese wear on the crown of the head, and turn backwards; for, to go without it is with them a sign that they have renounced the world. Then, being stripped of secular attire, they were clothed in a long robe, somewhat like our own, and thenceforth they lived among us, having stated hours for daily prayer, examination of conscience, and certain days during the month for frequenting the sacraments. They were also to assist the Father who had charge of them in instructing the newly made converts. Meanwhile their conduct was well watched, and their proficiency recorded in order to decide their fitness for the duty which nearly all of them were willing to embrace. After having gone through this probation, John, although still very young, was duly admitted among the catechists; and his parents, who were admirable Christians, not only willingly presented him to the Church, but thought themselves supremely happy in having such a son. And indeed, as it were, to crown their joy, they had, a few years afterwards, the ineffable delight of seeing him a glorious Martyr of Jesus Christ, and thus obtained that consolation which we will have occasion to mention hereafter. Having been appointed as pupil and companion to Father Peter de Morecon (a truly zealous missionary), he went with him to the island of Scichi, and there dwelt a long time instructing children in the rudiments of the faith. From thence he accompanied the same Father to Ozaca, where we had a residence in which were, at that period, Father Organtino, Paul Michi, and James Chisai. The example and conversation of these experienced men, intensified little John's zeal, and he exerted himself to the utmost of his power in the salvation of souls. Indeed, the harvest was abundant in that region; for, there was a vast number of Christians there even in the imperial court itself; so much so, that the great officers of state and other princes coming thither, offered themselves and their subjects for baptism. But notwithstanding this auspicious state of things, persecution blasted our fairest hopes and led to the martyrdom of John, who was then only nineteen years of age. Heaven, however, granted him the happiness of meeting in Ozaca Peter Martinez, bishop of Japan, who administered to him and many others the sacrament of Confirmation. Strengthened and enlightened by the gifts of the Holy Ghost, he was thus providentially enabled to maintain the faith of Jesus Christ, and to sacrifice his life for that inestimable blessing.

X.

THE LIFE OF THE HOLY MARTYR JAMES CHISAI. BORN AND REARED A HEATHEN, HE IS CONVERTED TO THE FAITH OF JESUS CHRIST.—HE MARRIES AND REPUDIATES HIS WIFE ON ACCOUNT OF HER APOSTACY FROM THE FAITH.

James Chisai was somewhat older than John, and was born in the kingdom of Bigen, in the year 1533. It is indubitable that his parents were heathens, and that he himself was involved in the same errors till he attained his sixteenth year. It would appear that his childhood was passed (as is usual in Japan) in some Bonze educational establishment, where he acquired that singular elegance for which he was so distinguished in writing the Japanese characters. We may here observe that this remarkable people have no alphabet like ours, whose letters combined form various words; but, on the contrary, they express everything by a character peculiarly its own, and that is inapplicable to anything else. These characters

D

resemble curved and right lines huddled indiscriminately together, and are so complicated that it is all but impossible, even though they were less numerous, to preserve any recollection of the strange and fantastic form they exhibit; and yet they amount to some thousands. This, however, was the total of all that Chisai could learn from the Bonzes—a most pestilent class and deeply dyed in every obscene vice.

The memoirs that have come down to us say nothing of the precise time or year in which he arrived at the knowledge of the true God, and was baptized. Father Louis Froes calls him *a very old Christian;* and this designation, according to the usage of the times in which he wrote, meant those who were either baptized by the apostle St. Francis Xavier, or by the two companions whom he left in Japan when about to return to India. Certain it is, that he received at baptism the name of James, or *Diego*, which are synonymous among the Spaniards. Being advanced in life, he married a convert, and had of her a son, whom he called John. Some time subsequently this unhappy woman was perverted by the Bonzes, lost the little sense she had, abjured Christ, and relapsed into idolatry. James exerted every means in his power to reclaim her from her execrable apostacy; but finding that prayer and argument could not remove her obstinate prejudices, he turned her out of his house, and separated himself from her by a legitimate divorce.

XI.

HE RENOUNCES THE WORLD, AND GOES TO LIVE WITH THE FATHERS OF THE SOCIETY AS CATECHIST.—HIS TENDER DEVOTION TO THE PASSION OF JESUS CHRIST.

THUS released from every worldly tie, James bethought him of uniting himself more closely with God, and in fulfilment of a long-cherished desire to devote himself as best he could to a more perfect life in the Society. Having, therefore, arranged all domestic affairs, and placed his son, as I think, in one of our seminaries, he requested to be admitted among our *Catechists*. His prayer was granted; and here let us observe that he and the holy martyr John, are not to be confounded with mere laybrothers or as we call them *temporal coadjutors*, to which grade they did not belong. This is placed beyond all doubt by the catalogue of informations which the superiors in Japan sent annually to the General, and also by the Bollandists, who say that Father Mutio Vitelleschi caused to be suppressed all printed documents in which these holy martyrs were styled laybrothers. Our James was therefore a *Dogico* or catechist, and consequently ranked among those who were promoted to the study of languages, or of the more advanced sciences till being sufficiently provided with knowledge, and strengthened in virtue, they were either ordained priests or from choice remained catechists to the end of their lives. In fine, a long report sent to Rome by Father Gomez, Viceprovincial, states that, James laboured many years with fervent spirit and untiring zeal for the conversion of the heathens, preparing them for the sacrament of baptism.

True it certainly is, that being somewhat advanced in years, and a man of singular humility, he took special pleasure in performing the lowliest duties in our houses. Hence it was that in Ozaca—where he passed the latest years of his life—he was employed to receive strangers at the gate, and to lodge guests—an office which he performed with that courtesy and urbanity so peculiar to the Japanese, and with that charity that so well becomes a true Christian. Every spare hour he had was devoted to meditation of our Lord's Passion ; and so tender was his devotion to this great mystery, that he derived from it renewed vigour, which enabled him to act the part of a truly sanctified man. Thoroughly familiar with the Japanese style of writing, he transcribed in that character the entire history of our Saviour's Passion; and this work of his, making a large volume, is truly beautiful for its illuminations, variety of characters and exquisitely coloured miniatures, finished with a master hand. And this book was his sole treasure—a rich pasture on which he fed his contemplative mind—a picture which he had ever before his corporeal eye of the Redeemer's sufferings. It also supplied him with good arguments to excite virtuous emotions in those who visited the residence to confer with the Fathers. In this sort of life he attained his sixty-fourth year, when it pleased God to exalt him to the honor of martyrdom, and to make him still more resemble his divine model, for love of whom he died on a cross.

SECOND PART.

PASSION AND DEATH

OF THE

THREE HOLY MARTYRS.

I.

FOUNDATION OF CHRISTIANITY IN JAPAN.—CHARACTER OF THE EMPEROR TAICOSAMA.

COMING now to the passion and death of the three holy martyrs, whose lives we have briefly described, it is necessary that we should go back to an earlier period, in order that the reader may be made acquainted with the causes which originated this first general persecution of Christianity in Japan. The Apostle St. Francis Xavier was the first to carry the light of the Gospel into that country, where he arrived in the year 1549, on the auspicious day of the Blessed Virgin's Assumption. Quitting those shores, he left behind him, to tend and cultivate the Lord's vineyard, Father Cosimo Torres and Brother John Fernandez, who accompanied him from India. As the harvest increased other zealous men hastened to their assistance; and portioning out among themselves those vast regions, which they traversed from centre to circumference, they performed miracles of zeal, converting kings and people to the law of Christ. The first among the princes to embrace it was Sciumetanda, lord of Omura, whose example was soon followed by Givan, king of Bungo, and four or five other principalities, and finally the king of Arima. These were the potentates who, as we have already said, sent ambassadors to Rome to tender their obedience to the Holy See.* During the reign of Nobunanga, whose victorious army conquered

---

* The embassy mentioned in the text reached Rome a short time before the death of Gregory XIII. who, on receiving the Japanese, exclaimed: "Nunc dimittis servum tuum Domine!" His successor, Sixtus Quintus, (who was crowned in 1585) treated the ambassadors with the greatest honor; and sent them back to their own country after a sojourn of some months in Spain and Italy. 'Tis said that they took two years to make the journey to Europe; and they were all under the guidance of Father Valegnani, who returned with them to Japan. The king of Bungo was baptized by St. Francis Xavier.— TRANSLATOR.

more than one-half of Japan, the religion of Jesus Christ was wonderfully propagated in that distant region. After Nobunanga's death and that of the rebel Acheci, another adventurer, Fasciba Chicodono, usurped the empire. Born in the kingdom of Mino, of parents in the humblest circumstances, he earned a living by felling wood in the forests, and selling it for fuel in the city. Tiring of this sort of life, he resolved to strike out a new destiny for himself, and throwing down the woodman's axe for the sword, he performed prodigies of valour, and began to ascend at a rapid pace from the lowliest grade to the climax of military honours, and was finally made commander-in-chief of the imperial armies. Finding Japan in a state of anarchy after Acheci's death, he dexterously seized the opportunity which was thus given him, and to such good account did he turn it that, after getting rid of Nobunanga's children and other adversaries who ambitioned supreme power, he, in less than a year, consolidated the Japanese under one monarchy, the kings and chief nobility of the country casting themselves like trembling vassals at his feet. He now assumed his old name, Fasciba, till 1585, when, as it were to make people forget his origin, he took the title of Cambacudono, which signifies the *ark of treasure.* At length, in the year 1592, he abdicated, in favour of his nephew, the dignity of Cambacu, and adopted the more august designation of Taicosama, or *supreme monarch.* During his sixteen years' reign he was the Tiberius of Japan—a foul beast in his habits and a cruel tyrant in his government. Religion he had none; for he did not believe in the existence of God. He alternately persecuted and favoured the Bonzes and the idols; nay, at one time he loved the Christians and their religion, but that love was speedily turned into hatred, and he persecuted them remorselessly. This conduct should not be attributed to mere caprice or inconstancy of purpose; for, Taicosama was always guided by one fixed principle, namely, to avail himself of every circumstance that promoted his own sordid interests.

II.

TAICOSAMA'S FIRST PERSECUTION OF THE CHRISTIANS—ORIGIN OF ANOTHER AND MORE TERRIBLE PERSECUTION.—HE SENTENCES ALL THE MINISTERS AND FOLLOWERS OF THE GOSPEL TO DEATH.

DURING the first five years, in which he acted kindly to the Fathers, the faith made wonderful conquests in every region of Japan; so much so, that it counted more than two hundred thousand Christians. In fact, Christians had command of the army and navy, were the most distinguished men in the court, and occupied the highest places in the general administration. The army itself was almost entirely Christian, and the standard of the cross might be seen everywhere in the camps and floating from the masts of the ships. Not satisfied with giving the Fathers license to preach the faith, Taicosama would often go in person, attended by a small retinue, to confer for many hours with Father Gaspar Coeglio, the Viceprovincial. On the night of the 24th of July (1587), after having been a considerable time closeted with the latter in a place called Facata, the emperor returned to his palace, where he drank a quantity of Portuguese wine, and then summoned to his presence a Bonze named Jacuin—a shameless wretch who acted as caterer to his imperial master's revolting appetites. Jacuin informed the tyrant that the Christian women of Arima had indignantly refused to prostitute themselves; and seasoning his narrative with many inventions of his own, he launched out into a bitter tirade against the Christian religion and the Fathers who were propagating it. But this was not all; for, the Bonze set about proving, with perverse ingenuity, that the emperor would never be safe on his throne as long as he tolerated in his dominions a race of men who taught the people a law which must finally subvert the gods, traditions, and usages of the country. Taicosama, who was always filled with sinister suspicions, and now stimulated by lust and fumes of wine, got into a rage, and swore a solemn oath that he would utterly extirpate the

Christians. On that very night he pronounced sentence of exile against Giusto Ucondono, the general of his army; and on the following morning he sent word to Father Coeglio that all preachers of the Gospel must, within a given period, quit Japan, at risk of their lives.

" How," asks Father Froes, in his report of this fact, " could we think of abandoning so many Christians? Nevertheless, in order to give the emperor's rage time to cool, and to show some semblance of respect for his mandate, the Viceprovincial ordered us to assume the ordinary Japanese costume, and without making any demonstration, to go on as usual attending to our flocks. Furthermore, in order not to give umbrage, we carefully avoided erecting public churches, and raised in their stead private chapels in retired quarters, where we could celebrate Mass and administer the sacraments. Each of these chapels had attached to it a sort of saloon on the exterior where we might be able to meet and instruct the people; nor should we omit mentioning that at the very moment when the proclamation appeared, we were actually building a residence in Miako, and another in Ozaca, where there were four fathers and six laybrothers. Owing to these precautions upwards of one hundred and thirty-four members of the Society continued to hold their footing in Japan, and in the meanwhile the conversions grew daily more numerous; so much so, that we baptized more than sixty-five thousand of the natives, without counting children born of Christian parents; and, yet, the emperor was fully aware that we were still in Japan; but seeing us live in such a retired manner, he had no desire to persecute us as violators of his law."*

Such was the actual state of affairs when in June, 1593, four Franciscans—two priests and two laybrothers—landed at the port of Nangasasky, commissioned by the governor of the Philippine islands, to treat as ambassadors with Taicosama about some claim which the latter pretended to have on said islands. They

* Apud Bolland. ad diem v. Februar.

were the first of all the other *religious orders* who visited Japan, and the principal among them was the Commissary, brother Peter Baptist, a man of holy life and truly zealous for the salvation of souls. On reaching Nangoia, they presented their credentials and gifts to Taicosama, and begged him to allow them to remain for some time in Miako. He consented, but on certain conditions. These holy men were not long there when, seeing what an abundant harvest lay before them, they opened a house and church, and began to exercise their ministry openly, to the great benefit of souls. This gave opportunity to the heathens, and particularly to one Faranda, a renegade, who for his own gain had at first acted kindly, to denounce them to Guenifoin, governor of Miako, as violators of the imperial edict.

Happily, however, as it would appear, the governor, who had two sons and two nephews Christians, did not forward the accusation to Taicosama, and the friars were allowed to live there for two years unmolested. But towards the close of

1596, things assumed another aspect, owing to the wreck of the ship St. Philip, which, in its voyage from Manilla to New Spain, was cast upon the beach of Urando, on the coast of the kingdom of Tosa. There were two hundred and forty passengers aboard the vessel, of whom ninety-five were natives of Castile, and among them four religious of the order of St. Augustin, two of the order of St. Francis, brother Philip Casas (or of Jesus,) a choir-brother, and brother John Povero, a laybrother, and one of the order of St. Dominic. On hearing of the wreck, Taicosama, according to the barbarous usages of Japan, confiscated to his treasury all that remained of the freight; and to enforce his orders, he despatched to the scene of the disaster a man, named Mascita, who was one of the three lieutenants of that quarter. Now, it so happened, that while seizing the property of the ill-fated ship, a chart, describing the coast, course of the winds, etc., etc., fell into the hands of Mascita, who, on examining it, asked the pilot how his king had presumed to take possession of countries so far away from Spain; and when the pilot answered, "By force of arms," the perfidious lieutenant remarked, "How can that be, when you have so few fighting men aboard your ship?" To this the pilot replied—in the hope of either frightening or placating the barbarian, who had treated them so cruelly, and, as it subsequently appeared in the juridical informations, with a lie of enormous magnitude, and to the great detriment of Christianity—"Sir, we first of all send the religious to preach, and then comes the army to make war and conquests." With the inventory of the ship's freight and the chart in his possession, and the statement of the incautious pilot in his memory, Mascita hastened back to Ozaca, where he made his report to Taicosama. The barbarian did not require this stimulant to set him on his bloody work; for, the King of Tosa had already been exciting him; and above all, the Bonze Jacuin, who, nine years previously kindled the flame of the first persecution. Taicosama hesitated no longer, and having declared his fixed intention of uprooting the *accursed followers of Christ* from the soil of Japan, he despatched on that very night—the 8th of December, 1596—a command to Gibunosci, Governor of Miako, and, at the same time, another to Farimandono, Governor of Ozaca, to search for all preachers of the Gospel and their followers, and place them under arrest.

III.

ZEAL OF THE CHRISTIANS IN PRESENTING THEMSELVES FOR MARTYRDOM.—TAICOSAMA MITIGATES HIS SENTENCE AGAINST THE FATHERS AND THE FAITHFUL.

WE had then in Ozaca four Jesuit priests, who came along with the bishop, Peter Martinez, who had left Nangasasky the day preceding. Father Organtino, the superior of the whole body, having learnt from a Christian page, who was in the governor's suite, that the ministers of Christ were to be sought for and arrested, and that the emperor designed to uproot Christianity, thought it wise to leave two priests in Ozaca for the benefit of the faithful. To these he added Paul Michi, with his two catechist colabourers, John de Gotó and James Chisai; and having made this provision, he himself, accompanied by Father Francis Perez and the lay brother Paul d'Amacusa, set out at nightfall of the following day to assist the Christians of Miako, and to offer himself on the altar of martyrdom. No sooner was Taicosama's inhuman sentence made known (comprising as it did all those who professed the Christian religion) than the entire of the converts were seized with an ardent desire for martyrdom! Father Organtino, on reaching Miako, having been apprized that he was in imminent danger of arrest, filled with joy and nowise dismayed, wrote the following letter to Father Peter Gomez, Viceprovincial, then at Nangasasky:—" What I now state must be a subject of great and common joy to you, to the bishop, and to all the Fathers and members of the Society; for, on the evening of yesterday Maria, wife of the deceased Givan, received notice from Fascimi, through her nephew, that a few hours ago the king had ordered Gibunosci to put all the Fathers to death. These tidings were confirmed by Father Paul d'Amacusa, in this very house where he addresses us in the following words : 'Fathers and dearest brothers, the hour for which we longed has struck !—now we can lay down our lives for that living God who was the first to sacrifice himself for us.' Hearing this, we were greatly consoled, and set about preparing ourselves as best we could. One spirit animated us all—Fathers, lay-brothers, catechists, and servants : nay, every one of the Christians, young and old, proved what they really were, ready and willing to share our fate, and lay down their lives for the love of God.

Our first preparation regarded the immortal soul; and then, that we might present a decorous exterior, we put on our ecclesiastical habits, surplices, and stoles, desiring to appear on the occasion as it became sons of the Society, servants of God, and preachers of his law. The joy that God sent into our heart might be seen on our faces; and, indeed, I have not words to describe it to you. This special grace of the Holy Ghost, has, doubtless, been obtained for us through the continual prayers which, by order of our General, are offered by the whole Society for this province; nor should I forget the fervent prayers of your fraternity, who can so well appreciate our toils and the dangers that are closing round us. Were anything required to stimulate and sustain us, we could have found it in the fervor, joy, readiness, and courage exhibited by all these good Christians, men and children of every state and condition; for we could not help observing, that they manifested no fear or melancholy, when on the point of losing their substance, children, wives, nay, life itself. The greatest danger they apprehended was that some of their kinsfolk would stand between them and the glory of martyrdom; and foremost among them was that good soldier of Christ Giusto Ucondono, to say nothing of others of the first nobility; the two sons of the governor Geienefoin particularly, the youngest of whom, Constantine, could not be induced to abandon us. How shall I describe the other Christians? The noblest among them sent their people to visit us; nay, and wrote to say that they are ready to join us the moment the tempest bursts—to die with us, their Fathers and teachers. Doubtless, fervour and zeal like this must, in great measure, be attributed to the sacrament of Confirmation, which the bishop administered a few days ago in the city of Miako." And in the same strain many others of our Fathers wrote on this momentous occasion. But it will interest the reader to peruse a portion of a letter penned by the laybrother Vincent, a Japanese, who addressed it to our Viceprovincial. Such a document is worth publishing, as it throws light on the writer and the events of his time:—" When the news reached me in Nara of what was passing in Miako, I dreaded to tarry any longer there lest I might not be able to join my brethren on the battle-field; and such, indeed, was my haste, that I fancied I was flying in-instead of walking. On my arrival I was overpowered with regret at finding my desire thwarted; for, as I was going right up to the house, where the soldiers were on guard, the Christians dragged me away, stating that I was the person for whose arrest the Vicegovernor had strictest orders. I then hastened to join Father Organtino. I declare to you, very reverend Father, that this distinction that has been conferred on me,—namely, that of being specially sought for among the many preachers of the Society,—and the conviction in the minds of the heathens that I am in any way a servant of Jesus Christ, has rendered some service towards the propagation of the faith. This assuredly is the greatest honour I could receive in this life, nor is there any other that will gladden me more in the life to come, when I stand before the Divine Majesty. What I now wish most is that persecution may be my lot to the latest hour of my life. Had I been suffered to do so, I would have gone to throw myself instantly among those Friar preachers who were arrested; but as I dare not overleap the limits which obedience prescribes, I resign myself to the Divine will. News has reached here that the king does not comprise us in the sentence of death; this has been a source of joy to the Christians who are anxious for the preservation of the faith, but as for us we regard it as a disaster and misfortune. Nevertheless, as changes are constantly recurring—and indeed so rapidly, that what is ordered in the morning is counter-ordered before sunset—we still cherish a hope,—and nothing seems more likely—that Taicosama will sooner or later sentence us to death. Come what may—and I trust it may be death—your Paternity shall find that we will bear ourselves in our sufferings and latest agony with a constancy and fidelity which no words of mine could express. When we are slain, those in your district may expect a like destiny; and when we are all reunited in paradise, we will gladly sing each other's triumph. But should martyrdom be withheld from us of the Society now here and from the other Christians, bear in mind, I beseech you, that before God they have offered their lives in sacrifice, all being anxious to die for the love of Jesus Christ." Those, however, who on that occasion won the palm of martyrdom amounted to twenty-four, but two others soon followed them to heaven. This was entirely attributable to the exertions and good policy of Gibunosci, Governor of Miako. This man was an idolator, but withal a well-meaning individual—so far as one of his creed could be such—who, unasked by anyone, but wholly of his own accord, returned to Taicosama the very day after the sentence had been promulgated, so indiscriminately involving as it did, all the preachers of the Gospel and their followers. On arriving at the court, Gibunosci pretended that he did not rightly understand the exact meaning of the sentence, and desired to be informed if the friars who came in the Portuguese ship from China were comprised in the list of the condemned. "For," said he, " as the Portuguese do not come for the sake of conquest, but simply for mercantile affairs—a matter of great benefit to Japan—the case of those fathers is different from that of the others. He further remarked that as it was customary to affix a tablet to those who had fallen under the ban of the law, declaring the crime for which they were condemned, and the sentence to be carried out, he desired to know in what terms *our* sentence was to be couched (the accusation against us not being identical with that laid to the friars' charge) and why *we* should be put to death along with them. This affected misunderstanding was made still more plausible when he remarked that Father John Rodriguez, his own interpreter, the aged Organtino, the bishop, and the ten of Nangasasky entrusted to

the ambassador Valegnani had obtained
from his Majesty a special license to remain in Japan." On hearing this Taicosama, without demanding anything more,
determined that none but those who had
come from the Philippine islands and
their Japanese servants should be put to
death. Gibunosci then observed that
the Portuguese whenever they came to
Japan visited him, made him presents and
did him homage as king of that country,
and he at the same time reminded him
of the embassy, and gifts which were
sent for his acceptance by the King of
Naban (so the Japanese style the Viceroy
of India), but more particularly of the
embassy of Father Valegnani, adding that
the bishop Martinez had taken his departure a few days before. Hereon the
king, expressed himself in an excess of
tenderness that could not have been
expected from one so cruel and heartless,
stating that he was sorely troubled for the
sufferings of his old interpreter John
Rodriguez, and that he would despatch
some of his people with an assurance that

the former, his old man (that is Father Organtino), the Fathers of Nangasasky, the bishop, and those who accompanied him, should not be molested either in person or property. The church, too, in which they officiated for *the Portuguese* was to be respected. At the same time he gave all to understand that he would allow no preaching or interfering with the established religion, and this he forbade under the severest penalties. He further declared, for the guidance of the Governor of Nangasasky, that he would not suffer any of the Fathers to enter Miako, except in the capacity of ambassadors or in the retinue of the Portuguese, who were accustomed to visit the court whenever their ships visited the Japanese shores.

Astonished at this wonderful change which had come over the barbarian's mind, Gibunosci lost no time in despatching messengers to Father Organtino (then in Miako), and also to Rodriguez, who had returned to Nangasasky with the bishop, and at the same time to his lieutenant, empowering him to withdraw the guards from the residence and set the Fathers at liberty. But long before these happy tidings reached Nangasasky, or Scimo, a rumour had gone abroad, as is usual on all similar occasions, very greatly exaggerated, to wit, that ten of the Society who were then in the neighbourhood of Miako and Ozaca, together with the six Franciscans, had been arrested and put to death with the most revolting cruelties, thus crowning their labours and reflecting glory on their faith by martyrdom It was also noised about that there was a general search for Christians, and that no day passed without witnessing the slaughter of multitudes of them—in a word, that the sword was to be unsheathed speedily in Nangasasky, Arima, Amacusa, and Bungo—wherever the Fathers, churches, and faithful were to be found—and that the ministers of justice were coming to vindicate the law.

This rumour, as may be supposed, caused the Christians to give themselves up to constant prayer, austere penances, and public preparation for death. As for our Fathers, they went about preaching in every quarter with a zeal that was rendered more intense by the circumstances and times. Night and day they were indefatigable in their exertions to comfort the poor people. In the interval, a courier, despatched from Miako to Fazamburo, lieutenant of Terazava, and governor of these kingdoms, bearing Taicosama's decrees, reached Nangoia. Along with the ordinances already mentioned, the courier was charged with instructions from the king's cabinet ministers commanding Fazamburo to prevent the Fathers from preaching, and to forbid any Christian, the Portuguese excepted, to enter the church of Nangasasky. The lieutenant was also ordered to interdict anything like the free and public exercise of the Christian religion; and no sooner was he invested with these powers than he wrote polite, but earnest, letters to John, King of Arima, and Santio, King of Omura, beseeching them, as they valued him, and the welfare of Christianity, not to exasperate the Emperor, who, if he were so inclined, could easily expel them from their principalities, and utterly destroy the Christian religion in Japan. He then released the three Franciscans, who were imprisoned in the hospital of St. Lazarus, lodging them elsewhere in order that the Portuguese might not discover them; and he finally issued a proclamation, warning the latter to make no attempt to caryr them off by sea or land.

IV.

TAICOSAMA SENTENCES THE RELIGIOUS TO DEATH.—A CURIOUS INCIDENT OF ONE MAN SUBSTITUTING HIMSELF FOR ANOTHER OF THE SAME NAME IN ORDER TO WIN THE PALM OF MARTYRDOM.

AFTER the final sentence, which consigned the Franciscan friars to death, and the selection of the twelve, who were to share their glorious fate, had been published in Miako, nothing further was done in their regard till the 30th of December. This was owing to the ingenuity of Gibunosci, who postponed their execution, hoping, no doubt, that Taicosama's rage would eventually cool. In fact, he flattered himself with the hope of being able at some favourable moment to persuade the king to deal leniently with the religious by sending them back to the place whence they came, the more so, as most of them were known to be ambassadors from the Governor of the Philippine Islands. But the malignant Bonze, Jacuin, divined his motives, and anticipated them; for, on the aforesaid day, he waited on Taicosama, reminded him of all that had passed, inveighed against the negligence of his ministers, in executing the royal ordinances, and inflicting summary vengeance on the destroyers of the gods of Japan, and teachers of the *devil's law*, as he used to style that of Christ. Indeed, so did this impious idolator work on the evil passions of his master, that the latter became, if possible, still more infuriated against the Christians when the Bonze reminded him of his former determination.

Having summoned Gibunosci to his presence, the monarch commanded him, without further delay, to cut off the noses of those on whom sentence had been pronounced. Some of them were in Miako, and others in Ozaca, whither they were all to be removed. This part of the sentence having been carried out, they were to be placed on wheeled vehicles (a large placard being carried before them to announce their condemnation), and exposed to the jeers of the idolatrous rabble in the most frequented thoroughfares of Miako, Ozaca, and Sacai, till they reached Nangasasky, where they were to be crucified, and left in that state till their decomposing bodies should fall to the ground. Such, indeed, is the usage among those barbarians. This inflexible order banished all hope from Gibunosci's heart, and he instantly dispatched a messenger to his lieutenant in Miako, empowering him to remove the five Franciscans and the twelve Japanese, who were condemned to die with them, from the place where they were under arrest, to the common jail. This circumstance, indeed, brought about an event which caused many and many a one to marvel; nay, and to praise the mysterious counsels of God's providence. Let us tell it. The Franciscan friars had in their employment a Japanese, named Mathias, who acted as their providore and cook. This man was comprised in the list of his twelve compatriots who were sentenced to death, but on account of the duties he had to discharge, the soldiers permitted him sometimes to go out into the city to purchase provisions for the Franciscans. Now, it so happened, that Mathias had gone out to make purchases a short time before the officer came to remove the prisoners; and when the latter functionary read out the list of the condemned each one answered to his name, and willingly gave himself up to the authorities.

When, however, Mathias' name was called, there was no response; and the officer proceeded to search the house for him, calling on him, at the same time, in a loud tone to present himself. Close by the door, at that precise moment, there was another Japanese Christian of the same name, who had been condemned among forty-seven others, and who, when the law-officers had reduced the list to twelve, was excepted from the number of those sentenced to death. But God so willed it, that he should be there at that, for him most happy moment probably, because Heaven had special views on him, and thought him more worthy of the martyr's crown than his namesake, who was absent. Hearing the officers shouting out Mathias, Mathias! he at once stepped forward, and replied: "That is my name; but to tell the truth, I am not the person for whom you are searching; nevertheless, I am a Christian, and if you wish to take me, I willingly surrender myself into your hands." Nothing more was required, and they took him at his word, placed him among the condemned, and marched him off. It would have been a sight worthy of paradise, if the other Mathias had come in at this juncture, and appealed to the Japanese officer, to prevent his namesake from depriving him of the crown of martyrdom, as happened more than once during the subsequent persecutions, and successfully, too, for the party laying claim to that incomparable honor. But such was not the good fortune of the missing Mathias, nor have I learned what became of him. When the Christians heard of this strange incident, they could not help calling to mind what St. Luke has said of the Apostle, who was substituted for Judas, "*the lot fell upon Mathias, and he was numbered among the twelve;*" and, indeed, this remark was all the more appropriate, as the *elect*, of whom we have been speaking, counted only eleven, and wanted one to make up the number of the apostolic college.

V.

HOW OUR THREE, PAUL MICHI, JOHN DE GOTO, AND JAMES CHISAI, WERE COMPRISED IN THE SENTENCE OF DEATH—THE WONDERFUL DELIGHT WITH WHICH THEY ACCEPT MARTYRDOM.

IN a different manner, but not without the special providence of God so willing it, our brethren, Paul Michi, John de Goto, and James Chisai, were destined to take their place among the Martyrs of Japan. We have already stated that they were excepted from the list of those whom Taicosama had sentenced to death, and whom he subsequently reduced to twelve, these namely who came from the Philippine islands and their followers. But let us proceed. After the tyrant had somewhat mitigated his former sentence, the governor, Gibunosci, sent orders to have the guards withdrawn from our residence at Miako. Such, however, was not the case in Ozaca, where Farimandono was governor. This man had been rebuked efforts made in their behalf by Giusto Ucondono and the two sons of the governor, Guenifoin, who did their utmost to induce Farimandono's chief minister to set them at large. Avaricious and corruptible as the latter was, like the great masses of the Japanese, no amount of bribes could soften his stony heart; and, indeed, Father Organtino, on learning what these good Christian gentlemen had done for the release of the prisoners, rebuked them in a letter, and showed them how such intrigues might injure the cause of Christianity in Japan. At length, on the first day of the year, 1597, Brother Martin and his three Japanese, two catechists, and the third, a preacher, were sent, under strong escort, to Miako, where they were thrown into the public jail with the others. Nothing could exceed the joy with which our brothers were animated on finding themselves in such holy companionship; and it was, if possible, heightened by a letter dated Ozaca, from Father Peter de Morecon, congratulating them on their happiness, and lamenting that he was not sharing it along with them. But among that band of Christian heroes, there was none whose heart felt such delight as did that of Paul. Loaded with heavier irons than those which crippled the limbs of his fellows, he was, nevertheless, the most joyful of them all; so much so, that his companions could never tire of contemplating the heaven-lit brightness of his features, or listening to the words which flowed with such unction from his lips. During the whole of that night in the prison of Miako, he never ceased preaching to the jailors and the Christians—who could not be induced to leave him—of the immortality of the soul, the eternity of the world to come, the glory of the blessed, the passion and death of the Saviour; but above all, of the unparalleled and priceless happiness of dying a martyr for the faith. This, indeed, was the dearest wish of his heart—the grand object on which all his desires were centered; and so well did he express himself when discoursing of it that, eloquent as he was by nature, his language now smote the ears of all around him, like something that had never before fallen from mortal tongue. What delighted him more was the discovery of so many points of resemblance between the sufferings of our Lord and those which he was about to taste:—He was in his thirty-third year! He was to die on a cross, and to be pierced with a lance! His passion dated from Thursday, when he was ironed! He was to be put to death by his own nation, which he desired to save! and then, on the following Friday, even as Christ was exposed to the execration of the populace in the streets of Jerusalem, so was he to be led through the streets of Miako, with the sentence of death displayed, to the place of execution! All who heard his words wept bitterly, and each of them spoke wonderful things of him long after his death. What is more, two of his jailors privately promised him that they would become Christians, and this added to the joy which he experienced in the prison of Ozaca, where he had the happiness of converting, and baptizing with his own hand, six idolators.

VI.

THE JAPANESE EXECUTIONER CUTS OFF AN EAR OF EACH OF THE TWENTY-FOUR MARTYRS.—THEY ARE EXPOSED TO PUBLIC DERISION IN THE STREETS OF MIAKO.—AFFECTING INCIDENT OF AN OLD MAN RECENTLY CONVERTED TO THE FAITH.

AT daybreak of the third of January, the twenty-four having been taken out of the prison, with their hands tied behind their backs, and surrounded by a vast crowd of guards and people, were led on foot to lower Miako—for it should be borne in mind that the place is divided into two great cities, the upper and lower. Here each of the martyrs had a portion of the left ear cut off—some more, some less, according to the whim of the executioner; and this, indeed, was a spontaneous stretch of mercy on the part of the governor, as the emperor's sentence was that each of them should lose the nose and both ears. During this barbarous proceeding our Martyrs had beside them two most fervent Christians, who were martyrs as far as they could be such; as they found none to slay them, although they were ready and willing to lay down their lives. One of them was Nodaghensuchi Victor, secretary to the Governor of Ozaca, already mentioned. This good man could never be kept from Paul Michi, but clung to him with unfailing fidelity from the 8th of December (the day on which the persecution commenced), till the 31st of the same. Constantly at our martyr's side, he never left him, except when called away by domestic affairs; and he finally brought his wife and children to reside in the vicinity of the prison, determined, should our people be put to death, that he and his would be the first to share their martyrdom. What is still more surprising, he actually consigned himself to voluntary imprisonment in the same dungeon with Paul, and when some one said to him, " Is it *piety* that induces you to expose your wife and children to death? can you love them and act thus?" he replied: " 'Tis because I love them I act thus; for, by this means I will procure for them happiness far surpassing any that they or I could secure. They understand this, and because they love me as much as I love them, were I not to offer myself for martyrdom, they would bring me along with them to it, just as I am now bringing them. Now, should I die without them, who will guarantee that they shall be reunited to me in eternity?" On another occasion when one of the Fathers with whom he was familiar in Ozaca, asked him to take charge of a packet of letters, which he had written for general circulation among the Christians, and others for particular individuals, exhorting them to maintain the faith, and lay down their lives for it, if necessary, he met the request thus, "What! would you force me to live? would you deprive me of the opportunity of obtaining eternal life?" In fact, he regarded the Father's conduct (although it was meant well) as the greatest insult that could be inflicted on him, and with tears in his eyes, he added: "I never thought, my Father, that you would thus requite my love for you by rejecting me as one unworthy to share your martyrdom!" In short, the letters had to be committed to the charge of somebody else, and this truly heroic man never quitted our three martyrs night or day. Even on their way to the place of execution he was by their side, present at the cutting off the ears, and accompanying them when they were paraded for public mockery in the streets of the city.

The other Japanese to whom I alluded was Andrew Ongasavara, a teacher of equitation and archery—arts highly prized and cultivated by the natives. While he was residing in Ozaca, his ardent desire to die a similar death, on the cross, prompted him to feign that he was owner of the house in which Paul Michi lodged, hoping thus that if none but members of the Society would be allowed to share his fate, he would either be the only one or the first. But as the lieutenant had only inserted the names of John and James on the list, it occurred to him that the number would be soon increased, and he therefore remained constantly with them. Meanwhile multitudes of the people presented themselves for the same purpose, and among them, Paul Sachiondono, a man of most exalted rank, each and all of whom began to contest with each other who should have the happiness of dying with the Fathers, in case those then present were not accepted. Each urged his own peculiar claims, and energetically, but none more so than the good John Goto, subsequently one of the three martyrs, who, having obtained leave of his jailors to absent himself for a while, hurried into the presence of Farimandono, the governor, and told him " that his name was inserted in the list, and that it should not be cancelled; and finally, that he ought not be deprived of his cross, which others whom the accident of birth and fortune had made more influential, were anxious to take from him." He had previously written to Father Peter de Morecon, asking permission to follow this line of conduct, but the good religious did not give his consent. Nevertheless this was of no great importance to Goto, for God had already registered his name among the twenty-six who were destined for martyrdom. Meanwhile the contest for the heavenly honour was decided in favour of Andrew who was pronounced worthy of the foremost place. After him it was awarded to Victor, the secretary, and to the rest in turn. But Andrew would have his whole family share his high destiny; even his decrepid mother, wife and children, some of whom were mere babies. His father was the only one with whom he had any difficulty, and as the circumstances of the old man's case are very interesting, I will not omit mentioning them.

This man was of noble birth, verging on his eightieth year, a courtier from his youth, and well skilled in the use of the sword. Andrew, therefore, as may be imagined did not find it hard to induce the aged parent to lay down his life with him and the Fathers, and thus win the martyr's crown. But still there was a difficulty to be overcome; for, when Andrew told him that he was bound to accept death joyfully and on his knees, offering himself to God, with hands and eyes raised to heaven, nay, and with bended neck and arms stretched out for the convenience of those who were to fix him to the cross, the old soldier got into a passion which he mistook for zeal, and replied—" what! to become a martyr must I die like a coward? Am I to stand by and see our good Fathers die, slaughtered before me just as if I had never wielded a sword? and you, unworthy of your father and your race, is this the advice you give me? Kneel down for the executioner! bend my neck!" and with this, as he had only a poniard at his side, he hurried off to fetch a scimitar which he had not worn for many years, and on his return began to brandish it in the air, and make various passes with the weapon, of which he was perfect master. He then resumed, " I find that I am still able to handle it; let these idolatrous dogs come on, and be they many or few, they shall not lay hands on the Fathers or come within sweep of my trusty sword. I will hew them down till nothing remains in my grasp but the sword's hilt, ay, till my arms fall powerless by my sides. Then let them slay me, and I will die like a brave martyr." Having spoken thus he once more performed a variety of passes, just as if he had had his youth restored to him. Many Christians witnessed this curious incident, and although it was a time for tears, very few of them could help smiling. Andrew, indeed, was sorely grieved by the spectacle; for, he knew that no words of his could convince the old man of his error. Nevertheless he besought him with affecting humility to withdraw from Ozaca till the fury of the persecution had passed away, but this request was ineffectual; for the old man regarded it as a cowardly suggestion, and said: "A brave man should never think of running away; 'tis disgraceful. I will die, sword in hand, as a brave martyr should die." None but God could change the old soldier's idea—the only erroneous one he entertained—simply because he was a novice in the school of

Christ, and so familiarised with that of the world, that he did not know how to distinguish the difference betwen military and Christian bravery. And God was pleased to demonstrate it to him in such an effectual manner, that he had only to visit his own house in order to comprehend it fully. On his return home he found his own wife and Andrew's preparing for themselves, their children, and nephews, the dress which they were to wear, that they might appear becomingly on the cross, and the other members of the family getting ready the reliquaries and rosaries with which they meant to adorn their persons. Hearing the women settling among themselves the order in which each would be crucified; who first and who second, with what willingness and reverence they should kiss the gibbet, and extend their arms for the executioner; what words they should address to each other; nay, and animating one another and thanking God for allowing them to lay down their lives for love of Him—hearing all this the old man was astounded, filled with admiration for what he considered so far superior to mere natural courage, and in an instant felt himself so entirely changed, that he exclaimed, " Andrew is right! this is heroism with which I was not acquainted, and far superior to mine." So saying, he flung away his scimitar and poniard, and in their stead armed himself with the rosary, and joyfully prepared himself to die like his pious wife and kinsfolk.

VII.

FATHER ORGANTINO'S SENTIMENTS ON RECEIVING THE EARS OF OUR THREE BROTHERS—HOW THE MARTYRS COMPORTED THEMSELVES IN THE STREETS OF MIAKO.

VICTOR, the secretary, and Andrew (both of whom I have felt myself bound to mention with respectful brevity) clung faithfully to our three during their imprisonment in Ozaca, on their journey thence to Miako, and were present while the executioner was cutting off their ears. Victor also gathered up the pieces, and piously carried them to Father Organtino. On receiving them, the old man's heart was deeply affected; his holy emotions were legible in his features; and so abundant were his tears, and so affecting the sentiments to which he gave utterance, that all the by-standers wept. He exhibited the mutilated fragments to all about him, kissed them, pressed them to his face, and then raising them up, while his tears flowed fast, made an offering of them to God. "These," said he, "are the first fruits of our blood in Japan, after all the sweat and toil we have expended on it, during eight-and-forty years. These are the earliest offerings from Miako—plucked from the parent stems, which in a few days hence shall be engrafted on three gibbets in Nangasasky, to the end that others may cull flowers still fairer and more abundant fruit!" Then, reflecting on his own case, he continued, still weeping: "would to God, it were my good fortune to share their happy lot! Ah, that instead of

offering to heaven, with my hands, the
blood of others, mine own were shed,
that others might make an offering of
it!" Venerable, holy soul, these sentiments were worthy of you, who so often
stood in imminent danger of martyrdom;
and yet, as though heaven did not think
you ripe for that honour, it was your
destiny to see the wreath plucked from
your brow, and the palm from your
grasp!

Meanwhile, the twenty-four being
placed on eight cars—three on each—
(and ours were the last,) they were led
through the thoroughfares of Miako,
their inhuman conductors taking no heed
of the blood that streamed from their
ears. Let the reader bear in mind, that
this public parade is the greatest indignity
with which the Japanese can brand the
condemned; and, indeed, it is never
resorted to, except in the case of most
infamous criminals. To disgrace them
still more, they were preceded by an
officer, who carried on the point of a
lance a large tablet, whereon their *crime*,

and the sort of death to which they were doomed, might be read in capital letters. In our vernacular it would run thus :—" Whereas, these men have come from the Philippine Islands, with the title of ambassadors, and located themselves in Miako, preaching the Christian religion, which I prohibited, under strictest penalties, many years ago; and, whereas, they have built churches, and been guilty of other such outrages, I now command that they be put to death, and along with them the Japanese who have gone over to their religion. The twenty-four are to be crucified in Nangasasky; and, as I now repeat my former prohibition, let it be universally known, and obeyed by all; for, should any one attempt to act contrary to this ordinance, he and his entire family shall suffer the same penalty. In the first year of Cheicio, on the twentieth of the eleventh moon."

Owing to the dense crowds following and surrounding the condemned, the procession had to move slowly, multitudes of the people forcing their way up to the cars. All the Christians were abroad in the streets, and the roofs and windows swarmed with spectators, each one giving expression to their feelings—some of pity, others of scornful joy; and such was the universal uproar, that it was difficult to catch the words which fell from the lips of some of our most courageous martyrs. Among the most distinguished of the latter was the Commissary, Brother Peter Baptist, who preached to the crowd as well as he could in Japanese, and animated his own brethren in their own native Spanish tongue. The two Franciscan priests, who came from the Philippine Islands—one of whom had been only a few months, and the other less than a year in Japan—not understanding the language were silent, and most decorous in their deportment, giving themselves entirely to God in prayer. Of our three, Paul Michi preached while the other two, with eyes raised heavenwards, were wrapped in profound meditation, and presented an aspect so radiant with delight, that a gentleman of the court, named Romano—

who, in spite of the guards, forced his way through the posse to salute the prisoners—never forgot what he saw and heard in that momentary interview. Indeed, so great was the consolation he derived from it that he never afterwards could speak of the event without shedding tears. But the observed of all observers and the theme of every tongue were three boys from twelve to fifteen years old, into whose youthful hearts God was pleased to infuse a truly superhuman courage, with a view, as we may suppose, to teach the heathens that joy and noble bearing like theirs could come only from heaven. Undismayed by the shouts and mockery of the crowds, and heedless of the blood that streamed from their wounds, the three youths chanted in unison the *Pater and Ave*, and whatever other prayers they had learnt. Most remarkable of the three was little Louis, who was but twelve years old, and who during the entire of the journey to Nangasasky never changed a feature and never looked in the slightest degree disheartened ; in fact, he astounded the religious, who could not but derive consolation and strength from his example. This was the same Louis who, while in prison in Miako, was visited by an influential idolator, who came to offer him life and liberty provided he would abandon the faith. "Ah," replied the boy, "you, too, ought to embrace it; for, it is the only means of everlasting salvation." Further on we shall give greater proofs of this youthful zeal, enkindled doubtless by the Holy Ghost, who selected this happy boy before others to manifest the wonders of God's grace. Nor should we omit stating that the fervour displayed by the faithful was beyond all praise. Thousands of them besought the escort to take them into custody and convey them to Nangasasky to be crucified. When told that they were not included in the list of the sentenced they begged as a special favour to be allowed to mount the cars, in order that they might thus share the scorn that was flung upon the Martyrs in the streets of Miako. They, good souls, would fain be partakers of their triumph! The procession terminated. (and, indeed, it lasted many hours), the Martyrs were brought back to the public prison, where there was a vast assemblage waiting to see them. Alighting from the vehicle, Paul Michi warmly embraced, one by one, the six Franciscans, thanking them for the great happiness they had conferred on him, namely, that of being crucified along with them; and, indeed, so astounded were the heathens at witnessing the heartfelt delight which glowed in his features, that they gazed at each other as it were awe-struck, asking " what sort of people are these, and what sort is the religion that enables them to rejoice in the midst of sufferings, glory in disgrace, and long for death?" Well might they talk thus; for, never before did the Japanese witness such a spectacle, and in after times they were wont to speak of it in almost the same words.

VIII.

THE MARTYRS ARE CONVEYED FROM MIAKO TO NANGASASKY—INCIDENTS ON THE WAY.

At daybreak they were all mounted on horses and conducted to Ozaca, and thence to Sacai, the two largest cities that lay on their route. In the latter place, as in Miako, they were paraded through the public thoroughfares, exposed to popular execration, their sentence being duly carried before them, as we have already described. From thence they might have gone expeditiously to Nangasasky by the channel which divides the islands from each other (for, be it understood, that Sacai and Nangasasky are both situated on the coast); but Taicosama, wishing to overawe the Christian converts, and at the same time to show his lieutenants and governors how implacably he hated Christianity, and how determined he was to prevent its dissemination, ordained that our holy martyrs should make the journey by land. Thus were they conveyed from village to village and from town to town, in each of which a prison had been prepared for them according to orders forwarded by the executive. The places assigned for their detention were formed of strong stakes driven into the ground, and connected with each other by a sort of wicker work, resembling that of cages. Soldiers in great numbers mounted guard over them, and right before the entrance the sentence of death, written in large characters, was raised on the point of a lance. They set out from Sacai on the ninth of January, and on the fourth of the following month they drew near Nangasasky, after incredible fatigues, during a twenty-six days' journey, which was rendered still more painful by the cold of the spring time; for, strange as it may seem to us, those regions are covered with snow and ice at that season. Nor should we omit mentioning that they were, in many instances, treated with singular humanity by their guards, who could not but admire the joy with which they welcomed death, their charity to one another, and their profound devotion. When not engaged in mental prayer, they conversed with each other of God and eternity, and thus edified the heathens, who did not fail to recommend them warmly to the various escorts who took them in charge along the way. They were occasionally provided with horses, and whenever the roads were very bad, they were carried in a species of litter, quite common in Japan. Nevertheless, they had to perform a considerable portion of the journey on foot, and their limbs were swollen and excoriated by the bitter cold.

At a certain village of the kingdom of Amacusa they were committed to the custody of an idolatrous official, who hated the very name of Christian so much that he treated them in the most inhuman manner; for, not satisfied with receiving them badly, he flung them into a foul dungeon, which was far fitter to be a den for wild beasts than a prison for a rational creature. Seeing this, Paul Michi contrived to have an interview with him, and the result was that he not only softened his hard heart, but converted him from idolatry to the law of Christ. This, assuredly, was little short of a miracle; but let us hear how God was pleased to bring about such a singular change. Having assured the personage of whom we have been speaking, that the prisoners, *whether guarded or otherwise*, would never harbour an idea of escaping, he gave as a reason for this resolve that they were only anxious for eternal happiness, which was to be the reward of all their sufferings. "You can now understand (continued Michi), that ours is not an affected joy, but rather a deep sense of consolation, which has its source in our hearts. We are not criminals consigned to death for violation of the emperor's laws, and the only crime laid to our charge is, that we adore the one true God, creator of the universe, whom we love, and whose religion we preach. Taicosama, your emperor, knows not that religion; and he has, therefore, condemned us for announcing it." He then unfolded the law of Christ to the idolator, who listened to him attentively, till the unction of his words, and the force of his arguments so overcame the barbarian, and dissipated his prejudices, that he requested to be fully instructed in the Christian doctrine. At length he became a believer, and before the dawn of the next day he received the grace of baptism.

During the remainder of the journey they enjoyed very many privileges—for they were allowed to spend their time as they liked in prayer and spiritual colloquies, occasionally listening to one of their companions cheering them with an exhortation. But, while thus intent on their own sanctification, they were not neglectful of their duties to others. As for the Japanese brethren, they took every opportunity of writing to their relatives and acquaintances, exhorting those who were Christians to hold by the faith; and those who were idolators to hearken to it, and embrace it. We still preserve many of Paul Michi's letters to our Fathers, then in Miako and Ozaca, and each of them is full of that holy spirit which animated him. In one of his epistles, he requests that a devout picture, which he valued, should be given to his mother, who was still living, " in order," says he, " that it may help her to fix her heart on heaven, as I cannot be bodily with her. It will enable her to raise her thoughts to God, into whose presence I am going to beg consolation for her." He also wrote to his dear friends, Giusto Ucondono, Paul and Constantine, sons of Genofoin, Andrew Ongasavara, and others, who spared no exertions to obtain his release. Instead, however, of thanking them for their charity in his behalf, he gently chided them for endeavouring to deprive him of the crown of martyrdom, which heaven was about to place on his head. Never, never, during that journey, of twenty-six days, did he tire of preaching on the roads, in the inns, and doing all the good that lay in his power. His toils were amply rewarded; for, many of those who heard him embraced the

Christian faith, and were baptized. As for himself, he has left it on record, that during his twenty years' toil, he never effected so much good for Christianity, or with such consolation to himself, as God enabled him to accomplish in that last journey. "And now," so runs one of his letters, "that I am condemned to death, solely because I have preached the law of Christ, I will continue to preach it with my latest breath." And indeed, as we shall see hereafter, he carried out his resolution, at that consummating moment, when he turned his cross into a pulpit, and had for his auditors the vast crowd that came to witness his triumphant death. What a happy destiny was his! His heart, like those of his holy companions, thrilled with delight in expectation of the martyr's palm. But more fortunate than his associates, he was the only one who could preach in the Japanese language, in which, as we have already said, he was profoundly versed. What wonder if his zeal grew more fervent, now that the hour of his triumph drew nigh!

In fact, his preaching exasperated the Bonzes beyond our power of describing; for they remarked, one to another, that Taicosama had acted unwisely in parading these men from Miako to Nangasasky, thus enabling them to traverse one half of Japan, and address the people as they went along. "This," said they, "is not uprooting Christianity from where it was, but rather disseminating it where it was not. Nay, more, had they never uttered a word, their very example, and the joy that animates them, in prospect of the eternal happiness which, they say, is in store for them after death, would be quite enough to infect the people. The nearer to death, the greater their joy! What a madness to have allowed them opportunity for addressing the multitudes, whom curiosity brings out to listen to them!" Such were the remarks of the Bonzes; but they had not long to wait, till they discovered that they were, in some measure, prophets of results, which they contemplated with dread.

IX.

THEY ARE JOINED BY NEW COMPANIONS ON THE WAY.—THE MARTYRS ARRIVE AT FACATA.—LETTERS FROM THE COMMISSARY, PETER BAPTIST AND PAUL MICHI, ADDRESSED TO THE RECTOR OF NANGASASKY AND THE VICEPROVINCIAL.

IRRESPECTIVE of the many incidents that shed such lustre on the journey of our twenty-four generous heroes, there was one which, if possible, rendered it still more signally remarkable. We allude to the accession made to their numbers on the way, when they were joined by two new associates whom God most providentially set apart for the honor of martyrdom. Two pious Christians, one of whom was a friend to the Franciscans, and the other especially devoted to ours, made a voluntary offering of their services to the Martyrs during the journey. One was named Francis, and the other Peter Suchegiro. The former was a carpenter, and had been baptized some eight months previously, but the latter had been received into the Church long before his companion, and was an *old* Christian. Although especially attached to the Fathers of the Society, Father Organtino arranged that he should have charge of all the others, religious as well as lay brothers; and he accordingly placed in his hands a sum of money sufficient for their maintenance and requirements on the road. This provision was absolutely necessary, when we call to mind the distance they had to travel, the severity of the season, and the other difficulties which they had to encounter. But as for the money, it could not have been entrusted to any one more competent to disburse it wisely. These two men ambitioned equally the martyr's palm, but they could only *hope* to win it, since their names were not comprised in the list of the twenty-four, and that list was now finally closed, though many in Miako were urgently requesting to be inscribed on it. During some days they thought of little besides performing whatever good offices they could for the Martyrs, utterly unconscious that they were thus earning for themselves the same heavenly honour. One day, however, they were called aside by some of the guards who, annoyed at seeing their own countrymen paying such attention to the condemned, questioned them thus: "Are you also Christians?" being answered in the affirmative, the guards replied, "Well, then, Christians and *Tobiri* (a word which, in Japanese, signifies proselytes), you must join them," and thereon they arrested them and tied their hands behind their backs. Thenceforth, during the remainder of the journey to Nangasasky, they were treated like their companions, and handed over to the detachments appointed to receive them in the various villages along the route. Their thanksgiving to God for this favor—all the more prized because least expected—was, we need hardly say, fervent beyond description. Their only regret was that they, like their associates, had not had their ears cut off, and that they did not share the ignominy heaped upon the former when paraded through the streets of Miako. Then again, as they drew near Nangasasky, they were apprehensive lest the governor who was charged to see the sentence carried into execution on reading the list of twenty-four, and not finding their names there, might probably exclude them. But as this was one of those gifts which God has not subjected to human caprice, nothing could deprive them of it.

As for the governer of Nangasasky, although he was certified by trustworthy witnesses of the cause of their accompanying the prisoners, and of the arbitrary and treacherous conduct of the guards who arrested them, nothing could alter his determination of putting them to death. "As they have fallen into my hands," said this fanatical heathen, "I think it far safer to slay them now that they are in custody, than to enlarge them because their names are not on the list." Thus with their newly added companions our martyrs entered Facata on the last day of January. Many of the Christian inhabitants waited on them soon after their arrival, and nothing could excel the tenderness and affection with which they were received by the former, to one of whom, named Diego Cogen, an intimate of Paul Michi, the latter confided a letter to be sent with all possible speed to the Viceprovincial, Gomez. The same kind sympathizer was charged with another letter by the Commissary, Peter Baptist, which was addressed to Father Antonio Lopez, rector of Nangasasky. Both letters were written a long time before in Catacabe, in the kingdom of Bigen, but the martyrs could not find anyone to take charge of them till they arrived in Facata. They both contained one simple request, and that was that the governor Terazava would allow them to celebrate Mass and receive the holy Eucharist. The Commissary's letter ran thus. " Twenty-four of us have set out from Miako, and we are all condemned to be crucified in Nangasasky. Three of us belong to the Society of

Jesus; six to the Franciscan order, and the rest are Japanese, some of whom are preachers. I implore your Paternity to obtain permission from the governor that we may be allowed to receive the most holy Sacrament two days before our sentence is carried into execution. We also request leave to receive the bishop's benediction, and to visit the Fathers of your college, to whose prayers we earnestly recommend ourselves. Catacabe, in the kingdom of Bigen, the 16th day of Jan., 1597."

Paul Michi's letter runs thus: "We are sentenced to die on the cross. Let not your Paternity be troubled about us; for, through God's infinite goodness we find our consolation and joy in Him; and our only desire now is, that some day before arriving in Nangasasky (for when we reach that place it may be too late), one of the Fathers of the Society may come to hear our confessions. This is the more necessary since the Franciscan Fathers are not very conversant with our language, and we cannot, therefore, confess to them, as we would wish. It would be a great happiness if you would send us Father Pasio. The twenty-four* of us are now animated by the same desire, namely—to hear Mass and receive the Holy Sacrament, at least once before we are crucified. Obtain for us this favour from Terazava or his deputy in Nangasasky." Both Fathers submitted this request to the deputy, who gave them kind promises ; but, eventually, owing to some recent circumstances, he absolutely refused to keep his word.

The man who acted so faithlessly was the idolatrous Fazamburo, brother of Terazava—then absent on public business in another province—so that the former was commissioned by the imperial cabinet to see the sentence carried into execution. On learning, therefore, that the Martyrs were approaching he gave orders for fifty crosses to be got ready in Nangasasky; and as soon as the citizens (multitudes of whom were Christians) heard of this pro-

* This letter was written before they were joined by the two Japanese.

ceeding they began to ask one another "Why fifty crosses, if the condemned are only twenty-four? Are *we* to supply the twenty-six, in order to make up the deficiency? Can it be that God desires to show us that we are dear to Him? But who are to be the *chosen* ones? Can the deputy have received secret instructions from court to guide him in the selection, or can he act arbitrarily and give the martyr's crown to whom he pleases?" The Fathers—and, above all, Peter Martinez, the bishop—thought that they themselves were to be the happy victims, and their hopes were grounded on some letters received from Miako. Then, again, the Portuguese traders and the Spaniards who had been shipwrecked fancied that they were destined for martyrdom; and, indeed, every Japanese Christian, who had deserved well of the faith, was ready to assert his claims to a cross.

X.

DISCOVERY OF MIRACULOUS CRUCIFIXES, PRESAGING MARTYRDOM ON THE CROSS.

In the midst of this universal preparation for death the Christians were reminded of an ominous event which occurred seven years before, and the import of which was never made patent till now. Three short leagues from Arima there is a place called Obama, whither one Leo, a devout Christian, sent his son, Michael, to hew wood for fuel, on the vigil of the Nativity, 1589. The tree which the latter selected for his axe was withered, leafless, and held in great veneration by the heathen natives, who, on each recurring new-year's day, used to fasten its branches to their doors, to keep out, as they foolishly imagined, evil spirits. After lopping off a good portion of the branches, Michael was about to split the trunk when night came and compelled him to go home. Next morning, however, he resumed his work, and with two or three strokes of the axe divided the trunk into two equal halves; but who could describe his amazement when he beheld in its inner rind an exquisite crucifix—exquisite as the hand of painter or sculptor could produce—just as if it had grown there, incorporated with the wood. There, under his eyes, was the holy symbol of salvation with all its details! He gazed at it for a moment; and then, overcome by terror, flung down his axe, and ran off to bring his father to witness the miraculous sight. Intelligence of this discovery soon reached our Fathers in Arima; and, after visiting the mysterious cross, they made a deposition of all the incidents connected with that portentous event. Nay, more, they had the crucifix conveyed to their church; and Peter Martinez, bishop of Japan, caused it to be enclosed in a rich silver shrine. But, what rendered it still more venerable, was the virtue which God imparted to it; for, many were cured of various infirmities by touching it, and many were released from the power of the devil, by praying before it. Thenceforth, crowds of pilgrims from Bungo, Amangucci, and Miako, resorted to it by land and sea, nay, and rivalled each other in their pious anxiety to obtain a particle of it, or of the tree in which it was discovered. Among the earliest of those pilgrims, was king John of Arima, who, on beholding it, clapped his hands, and exclaimed: "'Tis it, 'tis it!" And then, addressing one of our Fathers, reminded him of a dream which he related to him six months before, and which neither of them remembered till now. In fact, the king dreamt one night that he saw two venerable personages standing at his bedside, and heard them reproach him gently for his tepidity, and his want of punctuality in assisting at the holy sacrifice, from which he often absented himself without good cause. Who those personages were he knew not, but their aspect proved that they came from heaven. They exhorted him to resume his early fervour, and follow the advice and direction of the Fathers; and concluded with the following announcement: "Know that a symbol of Jesus will be discovered in thy kingdom; prize it, for it was not made by hand of man;" and having said this they vanished. The king related this dream to Father Gomez next morning, and also to many others; and he himself derived comfort and redoubled fervour from the mysterious forewarning. But what the symbol was, where it was to be sought for, or whether it would manifest itself, neither he nor they could tell; and, in fact, till now, he had all but forgotten the dream. Now, however, when he saw the cross, dream and admonition came back on his recollection, and he knew that what he had heard was a prophecy, and that the sacred object before him was the symbol of Jesus Christ, and not the work of human hands, as was most manifest to all. In a little more than two years afterwards; that is to say, on the 7th February, 1592, the same miracle was repeated in Facunda, the territory of Santio, prince of Omura.

Indeed many other crosses were discovered at this period under still more mysterious circumstances; and each of the holy symbols was greatly venerated by the faithful who drew their own conclusions from such foreshadowings. Some, indeed, inferred that the crosses thus brought to light portended that the faith was about to triumph in Japan; others fancied that they were meant by heaven to supply the places of the sacred symbols which Taicosama caused to be demolished; but many who saw farther into the future, were persuaded that such signal manifestations—evidently the work of angelic hands—were signs of persecution and death on the cross—for it is thus the Japanese execute capital punishment. The latter was the more universally received conclusion, particularly as Fazamburo had given orders for so many crosses; but it subsequently transpired that this was merely an artifice of his own contriving to overawe the Christians. The deputy, however, deceived himself; for, far from terrifying the converted Japanese, Father Gomez, the Viceprovincial, found it necessary to moderate the over-ardent zeal of the multitudes who, in their anxiety for martyrdom, presented themselves to the barbarian, openly avowing that they were Christians, and prepared to die for Jesus Christ. Thus, indeed, did the Christians comport themselves in Nangasasky, Ozaca, Miako, and in short, throughout all Japan, everywhere proclaiming their willingness to offer themselves victims for the Redeemer's law. But to show how wide-spread was this holy desire for martyrdom, we will here relate two simple incidents which prove that even children of tenderest years were actuated by the same heavenly sentiments.

One night a distinguished citizen of Nangasasky and his wife were conversing about their approaching martyrdom, and making ready the apparel they wished to wear on the occasion, little thinking that they had been overheard by one of their children—a little boy, aged eleven—who, with a younger brother, was in bed in the same apartment, and, as the parents fancied, fast asleep. The child, however, treasured every word that fell from their lips, and when they ceased conversing, he sprang from his bed and coming before them said: "You are preparing to die for the faith, and why would you conceal your intention from me?" He then implored them to tell him candidly what they had resolved on, and they, either believing that they had been overheard, or wishing to ascertain how the boy would take the announcement, told him that they had made up their minds to die martyrs. On hearing this the child's joy became almost ecstatic, and he expressed himself thus: "I thank God for this signal favor, and I congratulate you and myself; for, assuredly, you will not die without me." Then remembering his little brother who was asleep, he pointed to his bed, and asked the father what was to become of him? The reply was, "He, you, and all of us will share the same blessed destiny; all of us will die for the faith." "Then, rejoined the child, "we will all go to paradise. ' I desire nothing more, my happiness is complete."

Another fact has been recorded of a noble child, aged five years, who, on learning that the heathens were coming from Miako to murder the faithful in Nangasasky, was asked by one of our Fathers what he would say if he were questioned about his religion. "I will tell them openly," replied the heroic child, "that I am a Christian." "But, then, they will kill you," observed the Father. "Be it so," said the child; "and here is what I will do," with this he flung himself on his knees and stooped his head, as though he were about to receive the stroke of a scimitar. "But," resumed the father, "while you are waiting for the executioner, and when you are on the point of losing your life, what will you say?" Here the poor child thinking that he did not know what words he should utter at such a crisis burst into tears; but being encouraged by the Father, he returned the following answer. "I will invoke the holy names of Jesus and Mary, till the executioners cut my throat, but if there be anything else that I should know you must teach it to me."

XI

VARIOUS INCIDENTS CONNECTED WITH THE MARTYRS IN THE VICINITY OF NANGASASKY—FAZAMBURO'S AFFECTION FOR PAUL MICHI—PAUL'S JOY AND FERVOR—JOHN SOAN AND JAMES CHISAI MAKE THEIR RELIGIOUS VOWS—RESPECT SHOWN TO THE MARTYRS BY THE CHRISTIANS—JOHN'S INTERVIEW WITH HIS FATHER.

MEANWHILE, our band of faithful champions had reached Sononghi (situated within the territory of the king of Omura), some eight or nine leagues from Nangasasky, which was destined to be their last halting-place in this life, and the scene of their glorious triumph! Of their own accord, and to show respect for the place of their martyrdom, they proceeded on foot for some distance—with difficulty, indeed, for their limbs were frost-bitten and benumbed. However, as the greater part of the remainder of the journey was to be made in boats, they acted thus for the reasons already assigned

During this short march—so painful and reverential—they were allowed to rest themselves by the wayside for some moments ; but Father Peter Baptist, the Commissary, had scarcely seated himself among his companions when he began to weep, as though some mournful memories had risen up before his mind. Observing this, the guards who, during the whole journey from Miako, had never seen the shadow of sorrow on the prisoners' countenances—nay, not even a single tear —began to jeer them thus:—" Ah, they now discover that they are not far from Nangasasky ! They now are thinking of the crosses on which they shall be fixed to-morrow. 'Tis one thing to contemplate death at a distance, and another to find oneself in the gripe of the executioner! They have now abandoned their joyousness for wailing!" So spake the guards, some of whom compassionated the Martyrs, while the majority of their fellows treated them contemptuously, fancying that the fear of approaching death was the cause of the Commissary's tears. On hearing and seeing all this, our Paul implored the Commissary to moderate his devotion and weep no more, as the rude men by whom they were surrounded mistook his motives, and attributed his conduct to cowardice. Thereon the Commissary did as Paul directed, and told brother Gonzales, who understood the Japanese language, to inform the guards that his tears were not caused by the fear of death, as they foolishly imagined. "Quite the contrary," continued the Martyr, "for why should I fear to sacrifice my life for an object so grand and holy—the salvation of souls? Tell them I have wept, because I came to Japan with the hope of being able to found a house of my Order among them, and now find I have not been able to realize my project." But neither then nor since has any house of his, or any other religious Order, been established in Japan, whose inhabitants, alas! are ignorant of God and the faith of Jesus Christ. The time appointed in the Eternal decrees, for enlightening that unhappy people, has not yet come. True it is, indeed, that the precious seeds of so much blood broadcast by innumerable champions of the faith— Europeans and Japanese of every grade and condition—lie there, as it were, dead, and down-trodden in the soil. True it is, that for a term of fifty years, after the events of which we are writing, the whole of that idolatrous region was deeply dyed with Christian blood. Nevertheless, it will one day fructify a hundred fold, notwithstanding the barrenness of the soil. But that shall not be till God turns his merciful eyes on Japan, and then, indeed, whosoever goes to tend the Lord's vineyard there, will find an abundant harvest, for which they will be indebted to the toils and blood of its first cultivators. Fazamburo, the deputy-governor, was awaiting the arrival of the Martyrs in Sononghi, whither he came from Nangoia to take charge of them, and escort them to the place of their execution. He and Paul Michi, we should observe, were very fond of each other; so much so, indeed, that Fazamburo often went to hear his friend discoursing on the mysteries of our holy faith. Now, however, he had a terrible duty to perform—the friend, whom he so loved, was consigned to his hands, to be put to death on an infamous cross. The very idea of it affected Fazamburo deeply, and he could not repress his tears. But our saint turned on him a look of delight, and said: "You have no reason to weep, but you should rather envy me my death, opprobrious as it may seem to you. Remember, that the only crime laid to my charge is, that I preached the law of Christ—a law somewhat known to you—and that my sole crime has been to save 'souls from eternal ruin, and point out the one way that leads to everlasting blessedness. Instead, therefore, of tears and sympathy which my death does not require, grant me as a pledge of your affection, what I prize most, time and facility to confess our sins, and receive the Lord's body and blood." To this the Commissary added another request, namely, that he would cause them to be crucified on Friday. Fazamburo granted all they desired, for as yet the suspicions to which we will allude hereafter had not warped his goodness of heart. On taking charge of the prisoners, the boy Louis, of whom we have spoken, arrested his attention; and partly through sympathy for the lad, and partly in the hope of attaching him to his suite—for, indeed, he was a boy of quick parts—he told him that he would save his life if he agreed to enter his service in the capacity of a page. Hereon Louis answered: " I am altogether in the Commissary's hands." Hearing this the latter said: " Tell him you will do so provided he allows you to remain a Christian, and pledges himself to keep his word." To this the deputy rejoined: "Certainly not, and the condition on which I would release you is, that you will first renounce the Christian religion and embrace mine." But Louis was not to be shaken, and he calmly replied: " On such a worthless condition as you propose I reject the offer of life. Would you have me barter eternal happiness for a few fleeting years of temporal existence? On hearing this Fazamburo turned away and proceeded to Nangasasky. In the mean time Fathers Francis Pasio and John Rodriguez were in search of him; for, on receipt of the letters addressed by our Paul and the commissary to the Viceprovincial Gomez, the latter lost no time in sending his brethren to wait on the deputy, in the hope of obtaining from him what the prisoners so earnestly desired. In fact Father Pasio and his companion had brought with them all that was necessary for the celebration of the holy Sacrifice, and a letter from the Viceprovincial, in which the latter besought Fazamburo to grant the Commissary's prayer. They did not, however, overtake him, for he had gone off by another road; and the guards who were only too anxious to get rid of their prisoners would not allow the Fáthers to see any of the martyrs. An exception, however, was made in favor of Father Rodriguez, whose title—interpreter to Taicosama—they concluded, justified them in allowing him to visit the

Martyrs. On being admitted to the prisoners Father Rodriguez tenderly embraced them one by one, and nothing could exceed the heartfelt affection which each and all of them evinced. The six Franciscans, and *our three*, with the other seventeen laics, burst into tears, but above all, Father Peter Baptist, the Commissary, to whom Rodriguez read the death sentence, a copy of which he had brought along with him. They wept, indeed, but theirs were tears of delight and consolation, for it would appear that the Commissary had only a vague notion of the manner in which he was to be put to death. Father Rodriguez further told him that the bishop, Peter Martinez, spoke of them in a sermon which he had some short time before preached to the Portuguese, and eloquently commended, as they deserved, the courage and fortitude with which they were about to glorify God in their passion. " Christianity," said the bishop, " has been wounded by their death and consoled by their unflinching heroism." On this the Commissary modestly requested him to tell the prelate what he had seen, and how ardently they all desired to lay down their lives for the faith.

Rodriguez then addressed himself to Paul Michi, to whom he gave the various messages with which he was charged by our brethren; informing him at the same time that they all envied him the blessed destiny which heaven had in store for him —that they desired nothing so much as to share his lot, and that they were all offering the holy sacrifice, their penances, and prayers to God for him and his two companions. Hearing this, Paul was greatly delighted, and remarked to Rodriguez that deplorable as was the actual state of the Japanese Christians, we (the Jesuits) were not in bad plight at the imperial court; and that his conviction was, that his death and that of his companions, instead of diminishing the number of the faithful, would rather bring over great multitudes to the Church. "Remember," continued he, "that during our thirty days' journey I was continually preaching, and listened to attentively. This will surely redound to the benefit of our holy faith. In the very prison of Ozaca I baptized six infidels, who pressed me urgently to do so, in order that they might hold in remembrance that they were born Christians in a dungeon, and regenerated by one, who was going to die for the faith which they embraced." One of the foresaid was a wealthy and distinguished military man, who subsequently visited Paul in Miako, and openly avowed himself a Christian. "These," he continued, " are indubitable signs that the faith has great power to bring the idolators to embrace it—a power which will, doubtless, keep the Christians from abandoning it through fear of present death." And, indeed, he spoke the truth, for his sole exertions won more infidels to Christ than did the labours of anyone else; so much so, that the converts far outnumbered those who, unfortunately, relapsed into idolatry. At last, Rodriguez embraced our other two, John and James, and promised them in the Viceprovincial's name that they would be speedily permitted to make the three religious vows. He finally told the two Japanese, who had come over to the faith during the journey, as we have narrated, that he congratulated them and their converted fellow-countrymen on their enviable lot; and then gathering all the Japanese together, he gave them, in their own language (of which he was thoroughly master), an exhortation worthy of his zeal, and suited to the circumstances of those whom he addressed. His words struck deep root in their good hearts, and, as we may imagine, afforded them ineffable comfort. At parting they all wept. When separated by the guards, who would not allow them to remain any longer together, Rodriguez rejoined Father Pasio, and proceeded that night to wait on Fazamburo in Nangasasky. The deputy, however, had changed his mind in the interval, and was no longer disposed to realise the promises which he had made to the Commissary and Paul Michi. Fazamburo's original intention was, certainly, to have the Martyrs conducted to Nangasasky and lodged in the stockaded prison, which he caused to be erected for them in that place; but remembering the more than fraternal love which the Christians cherished for one another, and that nearly the entire population of the city professed that religion, nay, more, that there was a considerable number of Spaniards* and Portuguese there at the time, it occurred to him that an attempt might be made to rescue the condemned. And, indeed, nothing could have been more feasible, had the Europeans and native Christians so willed it. What force had the deputy at his command to counteract such an enterprize, if it was once set on foot?

Reflecting thus, he resolved to follow the safer course, which was to execute the Martyrs on the very spot where malefactors were usually put to death, a short distance from the city, and on the high road along which our heroic band was approaching. Thus, he would be rid of

* The former belonged to the ship Philip that was wrecked, and the latter to the merchant vessels that traded with Japan.

them on the instant. He, therefore, lost no time in causing holes to be dug for the twenty-six crosses, which, in obedience to his order, were brought forth from Nangasasky; and he, at the same time, despatched officers to various quarters on the Martyrs' route, forbidding the people, at the peril of their lives, to leave their houses for the purpose of witnessing the crucifixion. The Bishop, the Fathers, Europeans, and Japanese, were all comprised in this interdict. Nevertheless, as Fazamburo wished to realise as much of his former promise as he thought prudent, he, on that very night, sent a message to our Fathers, stating, that unforeseen and serious circumstances prevented him from doing all that he meant to have done; but that Father Pasio and Rodriguez might come to the palace early next morning, when he would place them under the protection of one of his officers, who would be authorized to halt the escort while our three religious were making their confessions. The Fathers obeyed the summons, and as they were about leaving the deputy's presence, he desired them to inform the other prisoners that he would not grant them the privilege of hearing Mass or dying on Friday. "For," said he, "that is not a necessity but a consolation, and those who are about to die for their religion are sure of salvation." Nevertheless our two Fathers urged their request so earnestly, that he at last, with great difficulty, allowed them to be present at the Martyrs' death. With that they left the palace. Father Pasio set out to await their arrival in the little chapel of St Lazarus, which was situated in Uracami, not far from the place of execution, and Father Rodriguez, accompanied by the officer, hastened to meet them on the road, in order to inform them that they would be put to death at the next halting place.

They were now coming from Tochizo, whither they were brought by sea from Sononghi, and all of them, with the exception of the six Franciscans, had their hands tied behind their backs, and as it were

I

to prevent the possibility of drowning themselves (as the heathens foolishly suspected), they were made fast to one another by a rope twisted round their necks. Nor should we omit mentioning that they were not allowed to come on shore during the whole of that long inclement night, but were forced to remain on the deck exposed to the intense cold.

Father Rodriguez met them within a league of Nangasasky, and he instantly told the Commissary (who was obliged to ride on horseback) and his companions, all of whom were on foot, that they should prepare themselves for death, as they were now fast approaching the goal of their earthly pilgrimage. These holy men received the announcement with great joy, and gave thanks to God for the honor He was about to confer on them. "In fact," says Father Rodriguez, describing this incident, "one would have supposed that they were on their way to some high festival!" Having joined the glorious heroes, our good Father went from one to another, addressing a few but fervent words to each—words which were suggested by that God whom he loved so ardently—nay, and by that fervor of spirit which he beheld in the Martyrs. In performing this charitable duty, he had to encounter many a rebuff from the rude soldiers; and some of the most distinguished citizens, who, anticipating the arrival of the heroic band, made their way through the crowd to embrace them, were subjected to the same harsh treatment.

On reaching the church of St. Lazarus, the officer whom we have already mentioned halted the entire party, and our three brethren, with their hands tied behind their backs, made their confession to Father Pasio. At the same time, the two catechists John, and James, consecrated themselves to God by the three vows of the Society.

Meanwhile, when the news of their arrival reached Nangasasky, many of the principal inhabitants, the Portuguese among others, obtained Fazamburo's permission to visit the Martyrs, for the purpose of imparting and obtaining consolation on this august ocasion. The Portuguese, moreover, memorialed the deputy to appoint some other place for the execution ; for, that where criminals were usually put to death was, so to say, infamous, and nowise worthy of the grand event which was about to take place. There were also many crosses there with the rotting bodies of malefactors still clinging to them; and it was for these reasons that the Portuguese petitioned Fazamburo to allow our Martyrs to die in some spot more in keeping with their innocence. In fact, they pointed out a place for the purpose, where they meant to erect, at some subsequent period, a church, sacred to our Lady of Martyrs; and, in making this request, they acted according to the instructions of our Fathers, with whom they had preconcerted the whole matter. They also asked that the crosses would be erected close to each other, and that a certain order should be observed in crucifying the condemned, and this, as we shall see, was eventually carried out.

In fact, Fazamburo granted all that they asked of him, and affirmed that it pained him to have any hand in the death of these innocent men, whose generosity and fortitude he could not help admiring. If anything grieved him more than another it was the fate of his dear friend Paul Michi. Nevertheless, he had an official duty to perform, and he was bound to discharge it. "Bear in mind," concluded the deputy, "that if this duty had been confided to any other of Taicosama's officers, he would have dealt far more rigorously with your martyrs, nay, and with all the Christians of Nangasasky, not excepting the princes of Arima and Omura, over whose territories I exercise jurisdiction and command. In fact, were I so disposed, I might destroy them and utterly exterminate the Christians of their states." While the crosses were being removed to the new site, and the executioners were making everything ready, the martyrs, who were still in the church of Saint Lazarus, had more leisure to prepare themselves for death. The faithful availing themselves of the opportunity, came in crowds to visit and embrace them, each one recommending himself to their prayers, and imploring them to keep them in remembrance when they were in the kingdom of God, for assuredly their blessed souls were about to soar from the cross to paradise! Piety and veneration like this, though justly due to these holy men, was, however, intolerable in their estimation, and on hearing themselves called "Blessed and Martyrs," they instantly cried out, "no, no, we are sinners; regard us as such, and beseech God that our blood may suffice to wash every stain from our souls." Thus did each of them feel and speak. Three Portuguese cast themselves at Paul Michi's feet, and in that lowly posture strove to embrace his knees. Not knowing their language, he could make no reply, but the blood mounted to his cheeks, and told what was working in his heart; in short, he dragged himself out of their hands. His reply to some of his own countrymen, who were desirous of honouring him in a similar manner, was characterised by severity of look and word. "Why," he asked, "would you afflict me at this critical moment? Give to God these acts of humiliation which are ill-bestowed on me; and if you love me beseech Him to pardon me a sinner, for I am such. Implore Him to accept this miserable life of mine, which I willingly offer to Him on the cross as an atonement for my sins; and that it may be acceptable in His sight pray, I beseech you, that my cross and my death may be united to that of our Lord Jesus Christ." Nevertheless this holy man was so animated by the grace of God, that the fire which glowed in his heart was reflected in his features; in fact, he looked like one in an ecstacy, as he went about hither and thither addressing his Japanese companions, and the bystanders in their native tongue, and repeating what he had already confided to Father Rodriguez, namely, that their death would increase the number of the faithful and prove highly advantageous to the spread of the faith. He pronounced these words in a tone of such emphatic earnestness, that those who heard them concluded that the future must have been revealed to his eyes. As for the good old James, he too, was enraptured at the contemplation of his happy lot, for he told all those who approached him, that Heaven had bestowed upon him within the compass of a few short hours, two graces greater than which he could not desire. " Congratulate me, congratulate me," he repeated over and over, " for I am now a religious of the Society, and I am about to die in the service of God—a witness for the truth." He felt grieved, however, by the importunity of certain Christians who after embracing him, asked him for an old handkerchief that was fastened at his girdle, which they wished to preserve as a memorial. Well knowing that they would have regarded it as a relic, he refused to comply with the request; but as his hands were tied behind his back, he could not prevent them from carrying off what they so much desired.

The interview which the youthful John had with his father, when the latter came to give and take the last adieu, impressed all those who witnessed it with wonder and delight. But we should observe that neither on the present occasion, nor when they met again at the foot of the cross was there a single tear shed, or a word of sorrow spoken by any of the parties. And this was as it should be; for assuredly the youthful Martyr's foot was already on the threshold of heaven! The parent deported himself with fortitude, and listened attentively to John, who exhorted him to obey the law of God, and secure for himself everlasting salvation by living a good life. As for the old man, he implored his child, then in his ninteenth year, to die joyfully, and with that fixedness of purpose that was required of one who lays down his life in honour of Christ, and as a witness for the faith. "Your mother and I," said the old man, "envy you; and should it at any time please God to select us for the honour you are about to enjoy, we also will gladly give our blood for the same holy cause." John then charged his parent to wait on Father Peter de Morecon, doubtless for the purpose of being remembered in the prayers of that good man whom he (John) had long assisted in the office of catechist, and from whose example he derived that firmness and consolation which he displayed at this awful moment. All the Martyrs now caused the reliquaries and rosaries which they wore round their necks to be taken off, lest they might fall into the hands of the idolators ; but they retained the medals and other devotional objects to which indulgences were attached. Father Francis Pasio then embraced the six Franciscans and all his friends and acquaintances; and, with the aforesaid treasure in his possession, hurried back to Nangasasky. His chief motive in acting thus was not to thank Fazamburo for the brief respite he had given to the Martyrs, but rather to obtain his permission to be present at the crucifixion—a favour which the escort would not grant him. The deputy, however, gave the necessary license. As for the bishop, Peter Martinez, all his earnest entreaties proved ineffectual; for, Fazamburo told him that the presence of a personage such as he was, would exasperate Taicosama to the last degree. The prelate, therefore, as he could render the Martyrs no other service, sent them his benediction.

XII.

JAPANESE CROSSES.—HOW THE JAPANESE CRUCIFY THEIR CRIMINALS.—INTERESTING INCIDENTS RELATING TO THE TWENTY-SIX CRUCIFIED MARTYRS. —PAUL MICHI ADDRESSES THE SPECTATORS FROM HIS CROSS.

A SHORT time afterwards an officer arrived from Nangasasky with a letter signed by Fazamburo, directing that the condemned should be put to death instantly. On receiving this intelligence, our Martyrs, no longer able to suppress their joy, thanked God for the favour he had conferred on them, and gave free course to the holy sentiments by which they all were animated. They embraced and encouraged each other with the most affecting tenderness; so much so, that those who witnessed this most solemn scene were one and all moved to tears. The spot destined for the crucifixion was a gentle hill on the road-side near the sea-shore, and within view of Nangasasky. The level ground on the summit of this eminence, afforded ample space for the twenty-six crosses, which were to be erected side by side, and within three or four paces of each other; and Fazamburo, probably apprehending an attempt at rescue, ordered detachments of musketeers and halberdiers to occupy the greater part of the ground. Within some eight paces of the crosses, the men-at-arms were drawn out in two long lines, and they were all provided with heavy clubs for the purpose of keeping the space clear, so that no one should enter the enclosure except the executioners and Fathers Pasio and Rodriguez, who had obtained permission to be present.

The Japanese crosses, along with the upper transverse beam for the arms, have also a lower one to which the legs are fastened; not overlapping each other, or drawn downwards perpendicularly, but stretched wide apart, and right in the centre of the shaft they are furnished with a projecting bracket, on which the condemned is supported (just as on horseback) after the cross has been raised up and set firm in the ground. We need hardly tell our readers that the object of this latter contrivance is, to protract the life of the condemned in greater torment and agony. In this most barbarous capital punishment, instead of nails they use four rings, or manacles, fastened to the cross, two above for the wrists, and two below for the instep of the foot. The neck is secured by an iron collar; and they sometimes fasten the waist of the criminal to the gibbet either by an iron hoop or a stout cord. The arms are secured in like manner. Our Martyrs' feet and wrists were fastened by means of iron rings, while some had their waists secured with iron hoops, and others with pieces of rope. We have already assigned the motives for this most cruel arrangement; but it may interest the reader to know that the Japanese leave their criminals on the cross long after they are killed—till, in a word, decomposition sets in, and they fall, bone by bone, to the ground. Nor are we to suppose that they strip the condemned naked; on the contrary, every one is crucified in his own clothes, no matter how sumptuous the apparel. The condemned, moreover, are extended on the cross while it is yet lying flat on the ground; but when it is raised up and secured in its socket, they either leave them to drag out a few days of most intolerable life, or despatch them on the instant. In the latter case, they usually give the unhappy wretch one or two thrusts of a spear; first in the right side, so that the weapon's point may protrude immediately under the left shoulder blade, and the second in the left side, and coming out under the shoulder blade opposite, so that both weapons may be said to cross each other. The instruments employed in this horrible work, are long, broad-bladed, and very sharp; and, indeed, they seldom fail to reach the heart at the first stroke. As for the executioners, they are exceedingly expert in their abominable art, of which they are very proud, deeming it a grand thing to be able to destroy life with a single thrust. When, however, they choose to torture the victim, they are sparing of their science; and sometimes take special pleasure in cutting the arteries of his throat.

Surrounded by the guards, our Martyrs were now led up to the place where the crosses awaited them. But who could describe the fervour and joy with which they beheld the symbol of redemption? Some cast themselves down on their knees before it; some embraced it with pious affection—some with eyes raised to heaven, made an offering of themselves to God; and some, too, begged earnestly that they might be *nailed* to their crosses. Brother Martin on seeing the one destined for him, chanted in a loud voice the *Benedictus Dominus Deus Israel;* and the little Louis, whose tender heart was so full of

God, on learning from one of the executioners that the shortest of the entire number was meant for him, ran to stretch himself upon it, exclaiming, Paradise, Paradise! Fazamburo had given orders that the condemned should be treated with every indulgence by the executioners, when the latter were placing them on the crosses; and he further commanded that the executioners should despatch them with all possible speed. It was, no doubt, through some similar sentiment of humanity that the deputy caused the crosses of the Martyrs to be *planed*, for those used in ordinary executions were generally shaped out of the trunks of trees, rough and knotty, just as they were when felled. Nevertheless, there were instances of savage ferocity on the part of the executioners, one of which we will mention. Finding that Paul Michi, owing to shortness of stature, was not seated astride on the *bracket*, one of those grim functionaries set about securing him with a handkerchief to the cross, while another, to facilitate the hideous work, planted his feet on the holy man's breast, in order to press him downwards. On seeing this, one of the Fathers implored the barbarian not to act so inhumanly, but the Saint rejoicing at this new humiliation turned his eyes on the kind Father, and said:— "Let him alone, he is acting as he ought." All these awful preliminaries being completed by the executioners, who were as numerous as their victims, the crosses were elevated simultaneously, and secured in the holes which had been prepared to receive the lower extremity of the shafts.

The faces of our holy Martyrs were all turned towards Nangasasky, where every housetop and window swarmed with spectators, anxious to witness the tremendous spectacle. In fact, every spot from the foot to the summit of the hill that commanded a view of this sublime tragedy was occupied by crowds of people—numbering over four thousand—Christians and idolators, together with all the Portuguese and Spanish seamen, who could not be deterred by Fazamburo's proclamation. The infidels were attracted to the scene by curiosity, the Christians by devotion. And, indeed, it was a sight worth being witnessed by the entire Japanese nation; for, such of them as beheld it—enemies of Christ as they were—could not refrain from shedding tears. Nor could it have been otherwise; for, when the crosses were raised into mid air a celestial joy lit up the features of our holy Martyrs, whose serenity and jubilation seemed to be a foretaste of that heaven which was soon to receive them within its portals. There they hung in presence of the vast multitude, with eyes raised upwards, as though they were making an offering of themselves to God, each giving free course to the holy sentiments by which he was animated and sustained. The Commissary, motionless and silent, kept his eyes fixed on heaven. Brother Francis Blanc thanked God for the favour He had conferred on him. Brother Martin recited passages of the Psalms; and Brother Gonzales (a laic, from the Canary Islands), repeated, in an audible voice, the *Pater Noster* and the *Ave Maria*. Antonio, a youth, thirteen years of age, sang in plain chant, the *Laudate pueri Dominum*, which he had learnt in our school at Nangasasky where, after being baptized by our Fathers, he was educated and presented to us by his parents as a candidate for the office of catechist. Being, however, too young for such an office, and on that account not received by us, he subsequently devoted himself to the service of the Franciscans. Louis on hearing one of the bystanders telling him " to comfort himself in the Lord," gave evident proof that his heart was filled with heavenly joy; for, he motioned with his hands and feet as well as he could; and such was the rapture tingling every nerve and muscle of his frame, that he seemed to dance upon his cross. The idolators were astounded at the sight, and yet this lad had been baptized only ten months previously. Among the more remarkable of our Society was John de Goto, who, inflamed with holy charity, exhorted the companion whose cross was next his own, to firmness and constancy; and, indeed, such was the radiant joy of his features, that he was the observed of all. When one of our Fathers, who was standing at the foot of his cross, told him to be mindful of heaven into which he would soon enter, he replied: "Yes, yes, be consoled, for that is the dearest thought of my heart." Right before him, animated with holy fortitude, was his own father, who, as we have stated, accompanied him to the place of execution, and wished to be present at his death, encouraging him from a distance, as best he could, by gestures to persevere to the end in the same unflinching Christian heroism. This man truly deserves to be remembered for ever; for, on ascertaining that his child was dead, and reflecting that he was the father of a martyr, such rapture over-mastered every other feeling, that he forced his way through the guards, ran up to the cross and kissed it, plucked off fragments of his child's clothes, and then hastened with them home to his wife—a woman of rare courage and piety—who derived ineffable delight from such sanctified mementoes of victory.

But the spirit which animated Paul Michi during that last and grandest scene of his life entitled him to be regarded not only as a Martyr, but also as a truly apostolic hero. There, from that pulpit of the cross,—which, irrespective of all other circumstances, was itself a homily—surrounded by a vast auditory, he raised his voice to the highest pitch, and when universal silence was obtained, he addressed the spectators thus: " Hear me, I implore you. I am not a stranger; nor have I come from the Philippine Islands. I am one of yourselves; a Japanese, and a member of the Society of Jesus. I have been condemned to this cross, not for any crime, but solely because I have preached the law of our Lord Jesus Christ. And I esteem it a great happiness and honor to die for that law; and I thank the Lord for having thus crowned my labours. Now approaching, as I am, the close of my days, and in that condition which, you may be certain, would deter me from deceiving you, I here protest and declare that there is no other law, and no other way of attaining salvation, than that which the Christians profess. And, since that law commands us to pardon our enemies, and return good for evil, I pardon Taicosama and all those who have had a hand in my death. Nor should any one suppose that I entertain hatred or resentment to those I have named; for, indeed, my dearest wish and most fervent prayer is that they all, and with them the whole Japanese nation, may become Christians, and thus save their immortal souls." At length the crowning moment came, and the executioners, drawing from the sheaths—in which they usually carry them—their trenchant broad-bladed spear-heads, got ready to terminate their bloody work. As we have already stated, two of these functionaries were employed to perform this last act of inhumanity; and commencing with the first, they transpierced the sides of all our holy Martyrs in succession, despatching some with one or two thrusts, and nearly all with a few more. Fathers Pasio and Rodriguez followed the executioners to the foot of each cross, and there suggested to the holy victims what they should feel and say at that awful crisis. As for the latter, as soon as they saw the glitter of the weapons, they invoked the holy names of Jesus and Mary in a voice so strong and clear that they were heard even in Nangasasky. The slain died with these holy names on their lips; and these who were not yet despatched repeated them incessantly till they gave up the ghost. During this proceeding the guards formed in closer array in the vicinity of the crosses; but this did not prevent the Christians from forcing their way through the strong columns, for each and all of them desired nothing so much as to collect a few drops of the blood that streamed so copiously from our Martyrs' wounds. Some, indeed, gathered it in the hollow of their hands; but very many came provided with white spotless napkins for the same pious purpose. One of these deserves especial mention, for he took off his coat, and holding it up by the folds, did his utmost to collect every drop that ran down from Paul Michi's side. An Italian, named John Baptist Bonacina acted in like manner; for, not satisfied with collecting the blood that streamed from Michi's wounds, he also absorbed as much as he could of that of the other religious in a linen cloth, from which he expressed it into a phial that he afterwards carried with him to Macao. The guards, meanwhile, went about striking, indiscriminately, the spectators with their clubs, so much so, that many of the Portuguese and natives, were seriously injured by the blows which they received. But every effort to prevent them from carrying out their pious wishes was ineffectual, for they set little value on the loss of their own blood, provided they could obtain even a few drops of that of the Martyrs. At last, Fazamburo's anger was so exasperated, that he commanded his men to charge and drive the multitude back to Nangasasky. No sooner, however, had he and his troops left the awful scene, than the Christians returned to scrape the blood from the crosses—nay, and to gather up the particles of it that had fallen on the ground. They, also, tore off the clothes of the Martyrs, wishing to preserve every fragment as a relic; and such was their immoderate zeal, that they left the bodies half naked. Seeing this, the Procurator of the House of Mercy at Nangasasky, had them decently covered with mats, the most durable material that he could provide for the occasion.

This glorious martyrdom took place on Wednesday the 5th of February, 1597,—a day memorable in Japan, not, indeed, because these were the first to lay down their lives in the service of the faith, but because they were the first who were honoured by an apostolic indult with the title and office of Martyrs. Besides our three religious, Paul, John, and James, we had in training four married men, namely, Tacheia Cosimo, Thomas Danghi, and two Pauls, Ibarachi and Suzuchi; and that Peter Suchegiro, who joined the Martyrs on their route, and also two youths, Anthony, of Chinese origin, and one Ventura.

XIII.

CONCOURSE AND DEVOTION OF THE CHRISTIANS TO THE MARTYRS.—THEY ARE VISITED AND VENERATED BY THE BISHOP OF JAPAN, THE KING OF ARIMA, AND THE PRINCE OF OMURA.

WHILE the awful event which we have described was taking place in presence of the crowds that came out to witness it, all those who remained within the walls of Nangasasky, natives as well as strangers, mounted to the roofs of the houses, and filled every window that commanded a view of this triumph of the faith on the neighbouring hill-top. The bishop, Peter Martinez, beheld everything that occurred from a window of our college, as he himself asserts in a report that he drew up at the request of Brother Jerom (di San Leonardo), guardian of the Friars Minors. "With my own eyes," wrote the bishop, "I saw them elevated on their crosses, and I also saw the sheen of the spear-heads with which they were slaughtered. I witnessed, too, the vast multitudes of Christians and heathens who hurried off to gaze at this spectacle: and although, by reason of the distance, I could not see the other incidents, I heard, nevertheless, the exclamations of the people when the executioners had finished their work."

Idolator, as Fazamburo was, the heroism of the Martyrs and the piety of the faithful made deep impression on his heart; so much so, that he asked our Fathers how it was that when the spear-heads were unsheathed to slay the Martyrs, the latter sang songs of jubilee, and the Christian spectators wept. On being told that the crucified sang joyously because they were to win heaven by laying down their lives for the love of Jesus Christ, and that the Christians wept partly through compassion for those innocent men, and partly through a holy desire of dying a similar death, he was literally astounded by the answer. But he was, at the same time, greatly afraid that Taicosama would learn how much the Martyrs had been honored by the devotion of the faithful after he (Taicosama) had condemned them to undergo the greatest ignominy—exposure to popular execration, and finally death on the cross. Full of such apprehensions, Fazamburo published a proclamation, in which he threatened to destroy Nangasasky if the Christians did not keep within doors; and warned them, at the same time, that not he, but they, would be responsible for the consequences if they persisted in disobeying his commands. It would appear that he resorted to these harsh measures on account of the vast multitudes of idolators from Miako, Ozaca, and Sacai, who were then in the city for mercantile purposes, and who, on their return would, in all probability, relate what they had seen; and, indeed, should such intelligence reach Taicosama's ears, the latter would, doubtless, treat Fazamburo himself, as well as the narrators, with condign severity.

It was difficult, however, to ascertain from the conversation of the idolators who witnessed the spectacle in the vicinity of Nangasasky, whether their shrewd comments boded good or ill; for, such was their amazement at witnessing the conduct of the Martyrs, and the Christians in general, that they could not help remarking to one another—" What an extraordinary religion is this, which makes the merest children play with death as though it were a toy! What an extraordinary people are these, who go rejoicing to encounter death, no matter how terrible or ignominious ! And then, again, the others, instead of trembling at the torments that have been inflicted on their co-religionists, weep and long for the same ; nay, envy them !"

Meanwhile a rumour went abroad that the Spaniards had determined on taking down the bodies of the six Franciscan Martyrs from the crosses, with the intention of carrying them off to the Philippine Islands, and the Portuguese *our three*, in order to take them to Macao; but as soon as it reached Fazamburo's ears, the barbarian became almost frantic with rage. He therefore instantly ordered that the scene of the crucifixion should be surrounded by strong palisades, and that two detachments of soldiers should mount guard there day and night, and at peril of their own lives, prevent every one from removing a single body. He also waited on our Fathers and told them, if either Portuguese or Spaniards dared to make such an attempt in spite of his and Taicosama's orders to the contrary, he would inflict summary vengeance, not only on the them but also upon the entire Christian population of the nine districts, over which he exercised command and jurisdiction. It, therefore, became incumbent on the bishop to obviate such a public calamity as this must prove to the Christians, were the Europeans to persevere in carrying out their intentions—a calamity, indeed, that never could be counterbalanced by the devotedness of the good Spaniards and Portuguese. Besides, we were quite certain of obtaining, sooner or later, and without running any risk, not only the relics of the foresaid nine, but those of the whole twenty-six. The bishop, therefore, published sentence of excommunication against anyone who would presume to molest the guards or strive to carry away the bodies committed to their custody.

This wise proceeding appeased the deputy, and so assured the guardians of our Martyrs, that they relaxed their severity and permitted the Christians to visit and pay due reverence to their sacred remains. The bishop, Peter Martinez, was one of the first to avail himself of this indulgence; for, he was allowed to satisfy his devotion, by visiting the scene of triumph two or three hours after the martyrdom. Having ascended the hill, and approached the crosses, he cast himself on his knees, to venerate these sacred bodies; and we may regard this as the first act of public worship that was bestowed on the holy Martyrs. Nor was it only from Nangasasky (which, as we have already said, commands a view of the hill) that pious thousands came to do them homage: on the contrary, multitudes flocked thither from remote quarters, some three, some four days' journey, just as pilgrims do in Europe when visiting the bodies of Saints. And the Japanese Christians firmly believed that the bodies of our Martyrs were holy, and, as it were, to prove that they deserved to be so styled, there floating from the staff of a lance was the sentence of their condemnation, setting forth that they were put to death for the faith! Thither came John, king of Arima, and Santio, prince of Omura, the former with the flower of his court, and the latter with his wife and eldest sister. They visited them all, one by one, and took pains to collect every incident connected with their passion. They spent a considerable time in presence of Paul Michi, whom they both loved dearly, and whom they had often heard preaching. What is more, prince Santio had in his possession a letter written by the holy Martyr a few days before he was crucified, replete with salutary instructions and admonitions to remain faithful to God, during the whole of his mortal career. On receiving it, he placed it reverently on his head (for it is thus the Japanese show profoundest reverence), and kissed it frequently, for he now looked upon it as a relic of a Martyr.

XIV.

WONDERFUL SIGNS IN CONFIRMATION OF THEIR MARTYRDOM; AND, ABOVE ALL, HOW THEIR BLOOD BECAME THE SEED OF VAST NUMBERS OF CHRISTIANS.

THE various miracles whereby God was pleased to show that the death of these holy men was precious in his sight, served to augment the number of those who hastened to venerate their remains. Indeed, the birds of prey and wild beasts, that abound in that region, never ventured to profane the bodies of our holy Martyrs. Moreover, on the Friday night, immediately after the martyrdom, two columns of flame, after resting some time above the crosses, were seen to move and settle over our college and the church of St. Lazarus, where the Franciscans had been lodged. The blood of Paul Michi, too, collected, as we have described, by the Italian Bonacina, remained for many months quite fluid in the phial which the latter brought with him to Macao. Passing over other miracles, of which mention has been left on record, in the reports drawn up by private individuals, we cannot refrain from adverting to one which the Sacred Congregation of Rites has pronounced to be the *chiefest*—namely, that the blood of these Martyrs proved to be the seed of innumerable Christians. Taicosama, indeed, imagined that the crucifixion of these twenty-six would overawe the faithful, as well as idolators; nay, and that he would be able to sweep Christianity out of his dominions. But such was not the case; and the Bonzes themselves could not disguise their rage on witnessing results which they never anticipated. Before Paul Michi's sides had been transpierced, a renegade Japanese who was instrumental in bringing about the condemnation and death of one of our Martyrs, hearing the

Saint pardoning his enemies and praying for them, was so affected by the words that he burst into tears, and, embracing a Portuguese who was his sponsor at baptism, publicly renounced his apostacy and re-embraced the Christian faith. Nay, more, many heathens of Nangasasky who were present at the martyrdom, on their return to the city, asked and received baptism. In all quarters whithersoever the tidings of the blessed death of our Martyrs sped, so great was the enthusiasm of the people, that Father Gomez, the Viceprovincial, found it obligatory to write a treatise in Japanese, showing when it is necessary to profess the faith *openly*, and what the Christians should avoid and observe in that regard. In the same little work, he further explained everything relating to martyrdom—its high merit and the dispositions it requires. To this he also added certain maxims for the guidance of the Christians, such as when they were bound to surrender or conceal themselves according to the teaching of the holy Scripture and the Fathers of the

Church. In the course of that same year, 1597, two thousand one hundred and forty idolators of the nine kingdoms bordering on Scimo, and in the jurisdiction of the governor of Nangasasky were converted to the law of Christ; in the following year Taicosama died, and ten of our society arrived from China—among them Father Valegnani and the new bishop, Louis Secheira, successor to Martinez, who died off Malacca, on his voyage to India in the preceding year.

The first thought of the bishop and of Valegnani, was to repair the losses which Christianity had sustained. The Society opened thirty new houses. The seminary of Nangasasky for eighty scholars was re-opened; the demolished churches were rebuilt, and evangelical labourers were dispatched to disseminate the faith through the whole country. The seeds thus broadcast fructified a hundred-fold. In the course of seven months, Father Baeza baptized 32,000 heathens, and 9,000 more were regenerated in Amangucci, Miako, and other districts. Suffice it to say, that in two years, 1599 and 1600, the souls won over to the Church in the kingdom of Scimo exceeded seventy thousand, which added to the other converts throughout Japan, raised the number of Christians to three hundred thousand. In fact, had that season of comparative peace lasted a little longer, every inhabitant of Japan would have been baptized. But the most atrocious persecutions of Taicosama and the two Xongun, his successors, blasted all this fair promise, and multiplied martyrs by thousands—nay, and uprooted every germ of Christianity, as Bartoli relates in his History.

XV.

TRANSLATION OF THE MARTYRS' RELICS TO MANILLA AND MACAO.—ACTS OF THEIR CANONIZATION.

LET us now return to our Martyrs, whose bodies, after being exposed on the crosses for two months, became rigid, nay, and frozen by the intense cold which prevails in Japan during the winter. But as soon as the heat set in, the remains of our holy heroes began to decompose and fall in fragments to the earth. On learning this, Father Gonzales sent some Christians to collect the relics, which he caused to be deposited in various shrines, and placed in our church of Nangasasky. Some time afterwards, these of the Franciscans were translated to Manilla, in the Philippine islands, and these of *our three* to the church of the college of Macao, in China.

Meanwhile, before leaving Japan, bishop Martinez drew up juridical informations of the martyrdom; and in the following year Father Secheira, his successor, resumed the same work, and took the depositions of fifty witnesses. Having obtained *remissorial* letters from the Sacred Congregation of Rites, Apostolic Processes were instituted (in 1621-22) in Nangasasky, Manilla, Macao, and elsewhere from which three Auditors of the Sacred Ruota compiled the information to be presented to the Sovereign Pontiff. This was examined and discussed by the Sacred Congregation, which, on the 3rd of July,

1627, decided that there could be no doubt of the martyrdom and miracles of the twenty-six crucified; and that it was lawful, whenever it might seem good to his Holiness, to proceed with the solemn canonization of the same. After that, Urban VIII., entertaining the memorials forwarded to him by the Catholic sovereigns Philip IV. and Isabella, the cities of Manilla, Macao, etc., granted to the entire Order of St. Francis, and to the Society of Jesus, the faculty of celebrating, in honor of their Martyrs, the Office and the Mass on the day of their death. On occasion of this gracious concession most solemn festivities were everywhere held, and especially in Japan, then harried by a most dreadful persecution. Nor was God slow in illustrating the merits of his servants, by means of new favours and miracles wrought through their intercession. Indeed, I have now before me authenticated evidences of three sudden cures which were performed in Munich and elsewhere, by the invocation of our three Martyrs. Moreover, these holy men have ever since been honored in the

Acts of the Congregation of Rites, and in the apostolic indults, with the title of Saints. The day of their passion has been duly recorded in the Roman Martyrology; and, in fine, their proper lessons and prayers have been approved—their rite being raised to a double of the second class. Nothing further was required, save the extrinsic function of canonization and the publication of the supreme declaration of the Holy See, which the Holiness of our Lord Pope Pius IX. has thought fit to pronounce in this year, 1862.

XVI.

CATALOGUE OF THE RELIGIOUS OF THE SOCIETY PUT TO DEATH FOR THE FAITH IN JAPAN—BRIEF NOTICE OF THE BISHOPS WHO GOVERNED THAT CHURCH.

NEVER since the first centuries of the Church did Christianity encounter more terrible trials than those which the faithful of Japan had to endure during a period of more than one hundred years. Exile, imprisonment, chains, spoliation of their goods, nay, death by strokes of clubs, decapitation, and other horrors were the appointed portion of these newly converted Christians. Cutting them across with scimitars, crucifixion, and thrusts of spear-heads were, indeed, the *ordinary* modes of putting them to death; but these were all speedily abandoned in order to substitute torments more cruel and protracted—such as roasting them alive over a slow fire, plunging them naked in ponds and rivers, and leaving them to be frozen to death; drawing off their skin and flesh, nay, the very muscles and nerves with pincers; and then, when almost reduced to the condition of skeletons, hacking them into fragments with blunted knives; dividing the arteries of the throat with a reed, and this so slowly that the martyrdom in many instances extended over seven days; filling the stomach with water and then placing the sufferer under heavy weights till the pressure forced water and blood to spirt from his mouth; slow submersion in the sulphur wells of Mount Ungen for the purpose of boiling them limb by limb;

suspending them head downwards over dykes reeking with every sort of pollution, that they might thus linger many days breathing poisonous exhalations, all these appalling devices of barbarous ingenuity, we repeat, were heroically endured by men and women of every state, nay, and by tender maidens, little boys, and merest children. The three Orders of St. Francis, St. Dominic, and St. Augustin, may be proud of their sons who braved all these horrors; but our Society can count eighty of its members who were put to death by one or other of the tortures already specified, to say nothing of those who either died in exile or sank under incredible toils. I will confine myself to giving a list of the latter in these pages, referring the reader for every thing I must leave untold to the copious volumes of Father Bartoli, and to the catalogue which has been published by Father Anthony Francis Cardim.*

* Catalogus Regularium et Sæcularium qui in Iaponiae regnis ab Ethnicis in odium christianæ fidei sub quatuor Tyrannis violenta morte sublati sunt. Romæ typis Corbelletti 1646.

V. F., *Venerable Father.*—V. B., *Venerable Brother.*

THE SIX PRIESTS PUT TO DEATH BY POISON DURING THE PERSECUTION OF THE KING OF FIRANDO.

F. Francis Carrion, a Spaniard of Medina del Campo, put to death August, 1590, at Inchisuchi, aged 36 years.

F. George Carvagial, a Portuguese, put to death May 5th, 1592, aged 42 years.

V. F. Joseph Fornaletti, of Venice, put to death in Arima, April, 1593, aged 44 years.

F. Theodore Manteles, a Fleming, put to death 1593, aged 33 years.

We have not been able to ascertain the names of the other two.

DURING THE PERSECUTION OF THE EMPEROR TAICOSAMA.

S. Paul Michi, a Japanese, crucified, &c., aged 33 years.

S. John Soan de Goto, Japanese, aged nineteen.

S. James Chisai, Japanese, aged 64.

DURING THE PERSECUTION OF THE EMPEROR XONGUNSAMA.

V. F. John Baptist Maciado, Portuguese, beheaded in Omura, May 22, 1617, aged 37 years.

V. B. Leonard Chimura, Japanese, roasted over a slow fire, November 18, 1619, aged 44.

V. B. Ambrose Fernandez, sentenced to the fire, died in prison at Omura, January 6, 1620, aged 69.

V. B. Austin Ota, Japanese, beheaded in Firando, August 10, 1622.

V. F. Charles Spinola, a Genoese, burnt over a slow fire in Nangasasky, September 10, 1622, aged 48 years.

V. P. Sebastian Chimura, Japanese, burnt on the same day, aged 57.

V. B. Antonio Chiuni, Japanese, burnt the same day, aged 50.

V. B. Peter Sampo, Japanese, burnt in same manner, and on same day, aged 40.

V. B. Gondisalvo Fusai, Japanese, burnt on same day, aged 40.

V. B. Michael Xumpo, Japanese, burnt on same day, aged 33.

V. B. Thomas Acafoxi, Japanese, burnt same day, aged 50.

V. B. Ludovico Cavora, Japanese, burnt same day and in same manner, aged 40.

V. B. John Chungocu, Japanese, decapitated same day, aged 40.

V. F. Camilo Costanzo, a native of the kingdom of Naples, burnt over a slow fire in Firando, Sept. 15, 1622, aged 50.

V. F. Peter Paul Navarro, Neapolitan, burnt in same manner, in Scimabara, Novemb. 1, 1622, aged 60.

V. B. Dionisio Fugiscima, Japanese, burnt same day, aged 31.

V. B. Peter Onizuca, Japanese, burnt same day, aged 18.

V. F. Jerom de Angelis, Sicilian, burnt, in same manner, December, 4, 1623, aged 56.

V. B. Simon Iempo, Japanese, burnt same day, aged 48.

V. F. Diego Carvaglio, of Coimbra, in Portugal, put to death in a frozen pond, in Sendai, Feb. 22, 1624, aged 46.

V. F. Francis Paceco, Portuguese, Provincial of Japan, and Apostolic Administrator of the bishopric, burnt over a slow fire in Nangasasky, June 20, 1626, aged 61.

V. F. John Baptist Zola, of Brescia, burnt same day, aged 51.

V. F. Balthassar de Torres, of Grenada, burnt same day, aged 62.

MARTYRS OF JAPAN. 177

V. B. Gaspar Sandamatzu, Japanese, burnt same day, aged 61.
V. B. Vincent Caun, a Corean, burnt same day, aged 46.
V. B. Peter Rinsei, Japanese, burnt same day, aged 38.
V. F. Michael Carvaglio, of Braga, in Portugal, burnt over a slow fire, in Omura, August 25, 1624, aged 47.
V. B. Paul Chinsuche, Japanese, burnt same day, aged 54.
V. B. John Chinsachu, Japanese, burnt same day, aged 21.
V. F. Thomas Tzuchi, Japanese, burnt over a slow fire, in Nangasasky, September 6, 1627, aged 56.
V. B. Michael Tozo, Japanese, burnt same day, aged 38.
V. B. Michael Nacascima, Japanese, after most cruel tortures put to death in the boiling wells of Mount Ungen, December 25, 1628.

IN THE PERSECUTION OF THE EMPEROR TOXONGUNSAMA.

V. F. Antonio Iscida, Japanese, who, after being tormented a whole month in the boiling wells, was afterwards burnt alive, in Nangasasky, September 3, 1632, aged 62.
V. B. Paul Niscifori, Japanese, burnt alive over a slow fire, in Nangasasky, July 22, 1633.
V. B. Nicholas Cheian, Japanese, the first put to death in the dyke at Nangasasky, July 31, 1633, aged 64.
V. F. Emanuel Borges, of Evora, in Portugal, put to death in same manner, at Nangasasky, August 16, 1633, aged 50.
V. B. Joseph Reomui, Japanese, put to death in same manner, same day.
V. B. Ignatius Chindo, Japanese, put to death in same manner, same day.

V. F. John Antonio Giannone, of the kingdom of Naples, put to death in the same manner, August 28, 1633, aged 44.

V. B. John Chidera, Japanese, put to death in same manner, August 29, 1633.

V. B. James Tacascima, Japanese, burnt alive over a slow fire, in Secchi, September 30, 1633.

V. B. Thomas Ricori, Japanese, burnt alive same day.

V. B. Louis Cafocu, Japanese, burnt alive same day.

V. B. Dionigi Jamamoto, Japanese, burnt alive same day.

V. B. John Iama, Japanese, put to death in the dyke, September 1633, aged 63.

V. F. Benedict Fernandez, Portuguese, put to death in the dyke at Nangasasky, October 2, 1633, aged 54.

V. F. Paul Saito, Japanese, put to death in same manner, on same day, aged 57.

V. F. John da Costa, Portuguese, put to death in the dyke, October 8, 1633, aged 58.

V. F. Sisto Tocoum, Japanese, put to death in same manner, October 9, 1633, aged 63.

V. B. Damian Fucaye, Japanese, put to death in same manner; same day.

V. F. Julian Nacaura, Japanese, a man of most noble family, who came to Rome as ambassador, put to death in the dyke, October 21, 1633, aged 66.

V. B. Peter, Japanese, put to death same day and in same manner.

V. F. Matteo, Japanese, put to death same day and in same manner.

V. B. Remigi, Japanese, put to death same day and in same manner.

V. B. Laurence, Japanese, in same manner.

V. F. John Adami, of Mazara, in Sicily, put to death in the dyke, October 22, 1633, aged 57.

V. F. Antonio de Souza, Portuguese, put to death in same manner, October 26, 1633, aged 50.

V. F. Sebastian Viera, Portuguese, Viceprovincial and Apostolic Administrator of the Bishopric, put to death in the dyke, and burnt in Jendo, June 6, 1634, aged 63.

Five venerable brothers, names unknown, put to death in the dyke with Father Viera.

V. F. Diego Juchi, Japanese, put to death in same manner in Ozaca, February, 1636, aged 60.

V. F. Marcello Francesco Mastrilli, tortured by infusion of water, dragged through the dyke, and finally beheaded in Naugasasky, October 17, 1637.

V. F. Peter Casui, Japanese, put to death by a variety of tortures in Jendo, August, 1638, aged 52.

V. F. Antonio Rubino, of Turin, Visitator, put to death in the dyke, March 22, 1643.

V. F. Alberto Micinsky, a Pole, put to death in the dyke, March 23, 1643.

V. F. Diego Morales, a Spaniard, put to death in same manner, March 25, 1643.

V. F. Francesco Marches, born in Nangasasky, whose father was a Portuguese, and mother a member of the royal house of Bungo, put to death in same manner, March 25, 1643.

V. F. Antonio Capece, Neapolitan, put to death in the dyke, March 25, 1643.

The Venerable Fathers Peter Marches, Provincial, Francis Casola, Joseph Chiara, Alfonso Orroio, and Father Andrew, a Japanese, were sawed alive in Jendo, 1644-5.

I have not included among these a vast number of Catechists, whom we were training as candidates for the Society, and who were also put to death by various most cruel torments.

Now, as to the bishops who governed

that once-flourishing Church, the first was F. Andrew, of Oviedo, a Spaniard, and patriarch of Ethiopia. Being obliged to live concealed in the mountains, on account of the persecution carried on by the schismatic Emperor, he was commanded by Pope Pius V. to proceed to Japan, in order to administer the affairs of that Church ;* but just as he was on the point of setting out, he was attacked by a serious malady, and died a holy death in Ethiopia. In his stead, the same Pius V. appointed Father Melchior Carnero, a Portuguese, who had been consecrated in Goa, bishop of Nicea, and coadjutor to the Patriarch of Ethiopia. He set out at once for Macao, in order to sail thence to Japan ; but, outworn by apostolic labours, extending over a period of so many years, devoted to the salvation of souls, he, too, passed out of this life on the 19th of August, 1583. On his demise, Pope Pius V. appointed, as first bishop of Japan, Father Sebastian Morales, Provincial of Portugal, who, after being conse-

* The Apostolic Letter is dated Rome, Feb. 2, 1566.

crated in Lisbon (1588), embarked for India. A contagious malady having broken out on board the ship during the voyage, the good Prelate, who spared no pains for the souls and bodies of the infected, caught the distemper, and died a martyr to charity, a short distance off the Cape of Good Hope.

The episcopal see of Japan being now a third time vacant, Pope Clement VIII. selected Father Peter Martinez, Provincial of India, giving him, as his coadjutor, Father Luigi Secheira, Lecturer of Theology in Coimbra. Martinez having been consecrated in Goa, sailed for Japan, and landed at Nangasasky on the 13th of August, 1596. He waited on the Emperor Taicosama; and subsequently traversed nearly all the principalities of Japan, adminstering the sacrament of Confirmation. He witnessed the martyrdom of the twenty-six crucified, and collected juridical informations of that grand fact. At length, having resolved on returning to India, in order to implore the Viceroy to give some assistance to his persecuted flock, he died at sea, off Malacca, in the February of 1598. On the 5th of August of the same year, Luigi Secheira disembarked on the shores of Japan. He governed that church sixteen years; and at last died, full of merits, in Nangasasky, on the 16th of February, 1614. After his death, the persecution raging fiercely, the Holy See determined that, during the widowhood of the church of Japan, our Superior then residing there should be, at one and the same time, vicar and apostolic administrator of that bishopric. Thus was Secheira succeeded in that office by Fathers Valentine Carvaglio, Francis Paceco, who was burnt alive, Matthew de Couros, who died outworn by toils, Sebastian Viera and Antonio Rubini, both of whom were put to death in the dyke, and Peter Marches, who, with his brother Francis, died Martyrs for the faith of Jesus Christ.

DECREE OF THE SACRED CONGREGATION OF RITES FOR THE CANONIZATION OF THE TWENTY-SIX MARTYRS.

Causa Canonizationis viginti sex Martyrum in Iapone de mandato regni illius Imperatoris pro Christi fide interemptorum, post relationem a tribus Rotæ Auditoribus tam Sanctissimo quam Sacræ Rituum Congregationi factam, plene matureque per plures sessiones discussa, referente Illustrissimo Cardinali Muto, ac cognito distincte, primum de validitate Processuum, deinde de Martyrio atque Miraculis; eadem Sacra Rituum Congregatio censuit et declaravit, posse, quandocumque Sanctissimo placuerit, ad præfatorum viginti sex Martyrum solemnem Canonizationem deveniri, et in Sanctorum numerum cooptari, et ut tales in Ecclesia Dei ab omnibus colendos et venerandos esse decerni.

Die 3 Iulii 1627.

Io. BAPTISTA *Card.* DETUS,
I. Thessalonicen, Secret.

DECREE OF THE HOLINESS OF OUR LORD PIUS IX., SANCTIONING THE CANONIZATION OF THE THREE MARTYRS OF THE SOCIETY OF JESUS.

Præter fortissimos illos viginti tres Athletas ex Ordine Minorum Sancti Francisci, qui animam suam perdere propter Evangelium haud metuentes, eam in æternam vitam custodierunt, alii tres æque præstantissimi fuere Viri e Societate Iesu, quos una cum aliis Ecclesia Iaponensis veluti Martyrum primitias Christo Martyrum Principi obtulit. Nomina illis erant Paulus Michi, Ioannes Soan, seu de Goto, utpote ex illa insula oriundus, et Iacobus vel Didagus Chisai Iaponenses omnes. Primus nobilibus ortus parentibus, subtiliori mentis acumine præditus, et Sacerdotio initiandus, qua scriptis, qua concionibus propogandæ fidei inter cives operam sedulo navabat. Alter litterarum studiis incumbens populum ad divinam legem erudire satagebat. Tertius rei domesticæ addictus quotidie Christi passionem meditabatur. In illo persecutionis æstu a lo Gubernatoris Ozacensis capti fuerunt a lict ibus in illius civitatis diversorio, licet tyrannus T. osama Patres Societatis Iesu in hoc capitali iudicio minime comprehendi declarasset. Hinc Meacum deducti, ibi cum cæteris Confessoribus in vincula publica coniiciuntur. Denique unicuique eorum auriculæ parte excisa, et per summum ludibrium in varias Imperii civitates circumducti, Nangasaquium usque perducuntur. Ubi paratis in colle crucibus, quas ipsi antea venerabundi salutaverunt, affiguntur. Paulus Michi ex illa triumphali cathedra ad circumfusam multitudinem pro Christi religione peroravit; illud palam sibi gratulatus, quod in cruce ut Christus Dominus, eademque, atque ille, ætate supremum expleret diem: donec singuli ab imis lateribus ad humeros binis lanceis transfixi victrices animas Cœlo inserendas emisere Nonis Februarii anni MDXCVII.

Posteaquam de hisce tribus Martyribus, sicut de aliis cæteris a Sedis Apostolicæ Delegatis instructæ fuissent tabulæ processuales, ac tres Rotæ Auditores iuxta vetustiorem disciplinam Causæ huius accuratissimam exposuissent relationem, Congregatio Sanctæ Romanæ Ecclesiæ Cardinalium, Sacris Ritibus tuendis præposita, suam aperuit sententiam asserens Constare de Martyrio et Miraculis, ideoque ad actualem illorum Martyrum Canonizationem quandocumque deveniri posse. Hinc Urbanus VIII. sa. me. qui iam Præsidi Ordinis Minorum Sancti Francisci de Cardinalium consilio Officium recitandi Missamque celebrandi pro tribus et viginti suis Martyribus facultatem fuerat impertitus in Litteris Apostolicis in forma Brevis XVIII Kalendas Octobris anni MDCXXVII expeditis, annuens etiam precibus

Præpositi Generalis et Presbyterorum Societatis Iesu, eamdem ipsis tribuit facultatem, Romæ editis insequenti die nimirum XVII Kalendas eorumden mensis et anni.

Verum Deus Omnipotens, qui congruam temporibus adhibere solet medicinam, permisit ut hæc præclarissima Causa pe tria fere sæcula subsisteret, ac nostris hisce temporibus ad exitum perduceretur. Siquidem erumpentibus modo undique Crucis Christi inimicis, ac fidei depositum penitus evertere conantibus, ipsi, qui in eiusdem fidei testimonium sanguinem fundere et crucis subire tormentum non dubitarunt, starent pro muro Domus Israel et gliscentia errorum monstra comprimerent et propulsarent. Quapropter Sanctissimus D. N. Pius Papa IX. postulationes excipiens Præsidis Minoriticæ Sancti Francisci Familiæ, quibus eum adprecabatur ut decerneret tuto procedi posse ad Canonizationem viginti trium Beatorum Martyrum eiusdem Ordinis, audita sententia pro veritate R. P. Sanctæ Fidei Promotoris nec non expetito consilio Reverendissimorum Cardinalium Sacræ Rituum Congregationis in Palatio Apostolico Vaticano tertio Nonas Septembris anni MDCCCLXI. Decretum tulit Tuto procedi posse ad Canonizationem viginti trium Martyrum Iaponensium ex Ordine Minorum Sancti Francisci. Quum vero Præpositus Generalis Societatis Iesu preces Sanctissimo Domino Nostro adhibuisset ut idem Decretum promulgare dignaretur pro tribus Beatis eiusdem Societatis Martyribus, Sanctitas Sua, iterum expetita sententia pro veritate R. P. Sanctæ Fidei Promotoris, rursus Consilium Reverendissimorum Cardinalium collegit in eodem Palatio Apostolico Vaticano pridie Nonas Martias vertentis anni, in quo per Romanum Cardinalem Nicolaum Clarelli Paracciani Causæ Relatorem proposito Dubio—An tuto procedi possit ad solemnem eorumdem trium Beatorum Martyrum Canonizationem? Omnes Patres Cardinales affirmativum protulere responsum. Attamen Sanctissimus Dominus suam noluit declarare sententiam, ut in gravissimo iudicio tempus intercederet, quo fervidius divina exoraretur Sapientia ad impetrandum lumen et auxilium.

Tandem hanc statuit diem sacratissimam, in qua Virgo Immaculata Maria ab Angelo tam venerabiliter salutata Aeterni Patris Unigenitum catissimis meruit excipere visceribus. Divina itaque Hostia in privato Vaticano Sacello piissime oblata, postquam in ecclesia Sanctæ Mariæ supra Minervam sacro circumdatus Patrum Cardinalium Senatu Pontificali Missæ solemniter adstitit, in proximum euisdem ecclesiæ Sacrarium ad se accersivit Romanum Cardinalem Constantinum Patrizi Episcopum Portuensem et Sanctæ Rufinæ, ac Sacrorum Rituum Congregationi Praefectum, necnon Romanum Card. Nicolaum Clarelli Paracciani Causæ Relatorem, una cum R. P. Andrea Maria Frattini Sanctæ Fidei Promotore, ac me infrascripto Secretario, iisque adstantibus pronunciavit "Tuto procedi posse ad horum trium Beatorum Martyrum Iaponensium e Societate Jesu Canonizationem." Huiusmodi autem Decretum in vulgus edi, in Sacrorum Rituum Congregationis acta referri, Litterasque Apostolicas sub Plumbo de solemni Canonizationis ritu in Patriarchali Basilica Vaticana quandocumque celebrando expediri mandavit, VIII Kalendas Aprilis anni MDCCCLXII.

 C. Episc. Portuensis et S. Rufinæ Card. PATRIZI
     S. R. C. Præfectus.

Loco ✠ Signi

   DOMINICUS BARTOLONI S.R.C. Secretarius.

THE END.

www.ingramcontent.com/pod-product-compliance
Lightning Source LLC
Chambersburg PA
CBHW030820190426
43197CB00036B/638